AMERICAN SOCIETY FOR TRAINING & DEVELOPMENT

Self-Directed Work Teams

A Trainer's Role in the Transition

Understanding,
Supporting,
and Leading
the Change

Edited by
Ed Rose
with Steve Buckley

ASTD

D1596992

Ordering information: Books published by the American Society for Training & Development can be ordered by calling 800.628.2783.

Library of Congress Catalog Card Number: 99-73475

ISBN: 1-56286-129-8

Editor's note: We have done our best to provide accurate URL and email addresses in this book. However, because of the ever-changing nature of the Web, some of those addresses may change.

Author's note: At the time of this book's printing, Harris Semiconductor was purchased by a subsidiary of Sterling Holding Company LLC, a Citicorp Venture Capital, Ltd. investment portfolio company. The company is now known as Intersil Corporation.

Table of Contents

Foreword

Team-Based Organizations: The Employee as Expert

Jon Cordas and Michael Beyerlein

As the murky competitive waters of the almost-twenty-first century grow increasingly turbulent, a new form of organization rises to meet the challenge. This future organization can be embodied in a single word: *adaptive*. Rather than functioning as a giant machine, this company appears to be an organism—learning, growing, and evolving. Company sustainability is gained through responsiveness that depends on such characteristics as continuous quality improvement, a value-added customer orientation, flexibility, speed, and the ability to redesign radically and rapidly in response to environmental shifts. The key to the future organization's ability to evolve is the development and leveraging of human capabilities and the effective use of advanced information technology. As projects change, webs of partnership links emerge both inside and outside of the organization in a self-organizing tapestry of resource and information allocation.

The human element in the future organization is the most radical difference readily noticed by an outside observer. Based on advanced design principles, such as rapid redesign and participative design, relationships and roles companywide have been restructured to align with a consistent logic and underlying design principle of collaboration. Instead of organizing people to work differently in the same organization, the entire organization is redesigned to maximize functional effectiveness. Spheres of authority have been redefined, and work on all levels is performed by interdependent teams. All teams are based on common principles: quality, improvement, communication, congruent cultural values, and work processes.

Power has been distributed throughout the company. All employees within the organization are viewed as experts. Work process design is done by those performing the work. Such democratic and full participation produces a tremendous sense of employee ownership and motivation. Accountability, responsibility, and honesty are fundamental organizing principles at all levels of the organization. A climate of trust has replaced a climate of fear.

Functions within the organization remain the same, but have been redistributed. Upper-level management performs strategic functions, such as investigating the environment for best practices; scanning for market opportunities; and being guardians over the vision, direction, and purpose of an effectively functioning organization. Middle-managers promote cross-boundary communication and remove production roadblocks. Line-level employees design and monitor their own work processes, perform continuous quality and process improvement, and perform their own command and control functions. The different organizational levels act in concert in an accountable, functional partnership.

Investment in training in the future organization is viewed as strategic resource development, and the training department plays a central role. Training is employee-driven. Because team members are stakeholders, teams request the functional and interpersonal training and development needed to meet well-defined operational objectives. Although criteria are difficult to align with team needs, human resource departments are vitally involved in the strategic planning and execution of practices in recruitment, selection, appraisal, career development, and compensation that help transform the organization. In addition to those traditional roles, teams are supported in the areas of self-auditing, communications, HRD practices, business metrics, legal issues, and public responsibility.

This vision of the future organization is distilled from writings of the leading minds in organizational design, and these principles currently are being introduced at the world's leading companies. The direction toward a truly democratic, self-managing organization may represent a difficult evolution, but the HR department is vital to future transformation. This book by the team from Harris Semiconductor, *Self-Directed Work Teams: A Trainer's Role in the Transition*, represents a major step along this path, emphasizing many of the principles of the future, such as participation, communication, cross-training, empowerment, accountability, teamwork, self-management, and employee expertise.

This book was written to help HRD and training professionals succeed in their roles as key contributors to the transformation from a traditional organization with centralized control to an adaptive organization with involved employees. It provides an overview of the principles, insight as to how they fit together, guidance for implementing them, and examples of their use. Harris Semiconductor has worked at this transformation for some time and the lessons learned from its journey are presented here as a guide for others. The HRD and training audience is specifically targeted by the book for at least three reasons:

1. The authors have decades of experience in those roles.
2. There are many books now on transforming a business but very few focus on the needs of HRD and training professionals.
3. HRD and training have a strategic role to play in making the transformation effort a sustainable success.

For example, during organizational change, communication is essential to reducing employee anxiety and resistance. The HR department cannot provide only communications between management and workers. It also must use training as a change tool to build common cultural values. In addition, the training and championing of employee participation is often the crucial element to implementation and diffusion throughout the workforce. Those efforts alone can make or break the success of a carefully analyzed and crafted change plan.

Examples in the book of curricula developed to facilitate change efforts provide an excellent frame of reference for training departments. Also, in the equation where "adaptability = shared principles, vision, and values + empowerment and participation," the competencies that members at all levels of the organization must develop depend on learning that is stimulated by the opportunities provided by HRD and training. Transformation to a new way of doing business depends on a tremendous amount of learning.

The partnership of industry and academia seems to be a particularly valuable concept in this book. A curriculum jointly sponsored by the two partners can provide increased resources for industry and offer employees the skills required for effective teamwork. An excellent-quality academic–industry program can serve as a powerful recruiting tool for both organizations and as a springboard for continued employee education. Completing a basic team education program could offer a novice employee increased opportunity for compensation and access to new career paths. The team curriculum can be applied to all teams within the organization, and includes technical, interpersonal, business, and administrative development. Because each team faces unique functional and interpersonal issues, later training can be provided as requested by the team.

An adaptive organization depends on the development and integration of the expertise of employees in all areas of the organization. Everyone needs the opportunity to develop critical thinking, communication, and participation competencies. Middle-managers also need new competencies in team leadership, strategic leadership, and tactical leadership. Some teams need other tailored learning opportunities. Adaptability of the organization depends on everyone having the competencies to scan the environment, detect problems and opportunities, communicate ideas, take initiative, and collaborate on building new business and new ways of doing business. Adaptation means survival for a company in the twenty-first century. This book provides a great starting place for professionals in human resources and training who want to play an important role in transforming their companies so they can survive and prosper.

Preface

In 1990, Harris Semiconductor's plant in Mountaintop, Pennsylvania, was
losing $20 million a year and had laid off 45 percent of its salaried
workers and 25 percent of its hourly workforce. In March 1990, the company decided to introduce a team-based management system called
"Quality by Design," the forerunner of self-directed work teams (SDWTs).
Within three years, the plant was back on track and it posted its first profit
in 1993. One year later, its steady profits encouraged corporate management to invest $250 million in a new factory at the site.

Not only has the change been dramatic, but it has put Harris Semiconductor on the "corporate turnaround story" circuit. The plant receives
two or three requests for plant tours every week and its managers are in
demand as speakers for local organizations. Seventy-five applicants show
up for every production job, although the local unemployment rate is less
than 7 percent (Bishop, 1998).

That dramatic reversal of fortune was driven by a number of factors,
including smart business decisions, good timing, and the health of the
electronics industry. But to slight the influence of a team-based structure

would not be fair. An empowered and committed workforce acting together as a *team* is key to the creation and maintenance of any financially successful organization. The names given to such teams vary: self-directed work teams, high-performance work teams, self-managed work teams, among others. In this book, we will use the term self-directed to describe the teams, but you can use whatever term you wish as long as everyone understands its intent and purpose. No matter what you call them, the concepts and principles they embody create an atmosphere in which employees are seen as valuable resources.

Dozens of books have been written about forming, managing, and empowering teams, and we certainly will cover these topics. But this book is unique for two reasons:

1. We assume that your organization currently is engaged in efforts either to develop a team-based structure or to enhance an existing team structure.

2. We focus on the trainer's role in the transition to SDWTs.

We have used the terms "trainer" and "human resource professional" interchangeably throughout the book because we consider the terms synonymous. We believe that your role as trainer can be extremely important in the structural transition to teams. Our experience as a manager of training at Harris Semiconductor has demonstrated that fact, as have my 15 years spent developing, implementing, and managing in a team-based organization. The reason for sharing Harris's extensive practical experience in implementing SDWTs is to provide proven tools and techniques to help you through a similar transition. The basic concepts in this book have been presented to more than 140 companies around the world that have sought Harris's experience as a benchmarking partner for their own transitions to SDWTs.

As a further validation of the work that Harris Semiconductor has done with SDWTs, the company received the Leadership Excellence Award in February 1999 from the Work in America Institute, a national research organization studying the field of high-performance work systems. That award recognized Harris's team accomplishments, including the implementation of SDWTs, as well as cross-functional problem-solving systems, and efforts to balance work life with home life at the company site in Palm Bay, Florida.

Our goal is to share some of this success with the reader, along with tools, techniques, and practical examples for effective facilitation of the change to team-based management in your organization. It specifically targets the trainer's role and provides a grounding to help you discover that unique role. The book will also discuss

- the various types of teams
- basic principles for organizational change and how these principles tie to specific activities at Harris
- a six-step process for forming any type of team, including worksheets to help you train and develop the teams in your organization
- descriptions of training classes used successfully to enhance the development of SDWTs
- an action plan for organizational change and a discussion of your role in that change
- tips for avoiding pitfalls and hazards during the transition
- activities, exercises, and attention-grabbers to help trainers facilitate the change process.

We will share with you specific information about our journey to a SDWT structure. Section I focuses on change and how to implement a cultural change of this magnitude effectively. Section II addresses the training and leadership required for this implementation. Section III presents design guidelines and specific action steps formulated from our own implementation process. Section IV describes initiatives and exercises to help your organization through the transition process.

We hope this book successfully highlights the critical role of the training professional in the transition to SDWTs and serves as a worthwhile road map for your organization to follow during its implementation of teams.

Acknowledgments

This book is truly an example of teamwork in action. It was written from the experiences we shared and the lessons we learned during our transition from a traditional management structure to a team-based organization at Harris Semiconductor. Senior management support and the tactical role of the trainer were *critical* in our transition process. The spirit of the frontline workers and middle-managers faced with drastic change and their ability to implement the new structure contributed enormously to the success of the effort. In addition, it was the visionary leadership of the union members and leaders at our sites in Findlay, Ohio, and Mountaintop, Pennsylvania, that made the transition possible at those locations. We dedicate this book to the manufacturing employees of Harris Semiconductor sites worldwide.

This work-in-progress (since 1992) would never have become a reality without the consulting genius of Louis Martin-Vega and Steve Gilmore. Bill Levinson's unique perspective on the unionized facilities and his overall contribution to the project were invaluable. A great deal of the credit also goes to Ray Odom, vice president and general manager of Harris Semiconductor's space and defense division: through his visionary leadership the concepts presented here came to life at Harris.

We also thank Darcy Hitchcock, the only coauthor not associated with Harris, for her contribution to the project. Darcy and Ed Rose presented together at a national training conference on SDWTs, and she is well respected for her extensive knowledge of teams and the attributes that make them successful.

Ed Rose
Steve Buckley

Author's Note: At the time of this book's printing, Harris Semiconductor was purchased by a subsidiary of Sterling Holding Company LLC, a Citicorp Venture Capital, Ltd. investment portfolio company. The company is now known as Intersil Corporation.

Section I

An Introduction to Teams

Seven Rules for Continuous Business Improvement:
1. Fix it even if it's not broken.
2. Work smarter, not harder.
3. Keep your work processes simple.
4. The customer is the boss.
5. Take what is and create a variation that customers need.
6. Remember: Success is not permanent.
7. When on top, keep climbing.

— Ed Rose

Chapter 1

Teams, Teams, and More Teams

Darcy Hitchcock

The focus of this book is a trainer's role in implementing self-directed work teams (SDWTs) and subsequent chapters will concentrate on that training function. But at the outset it is crucial to note that SDWTs are not an organization's only strategic option. Your organization will want to employ a variety of team types, and to do so it is crucial that you

- clarify the purpose of the team.
- identify the most appropriate team type to use.
- use the best methods and tools for the team type selected.

A mistake in any one or more of those three areas will lead to failure. Do any of the examples below ring true for your organization?

Mistake #1: Confusing the purpose and picking the wrong team type. Operating under the misconception that all teams are alike can lead to practices that defy logic. A college assembled its department and program heads into a "team" to improve cross-discipline synergies. This management team (some 50 people) dutifully met monthly and tried to act like a self-directed team. The meetings dragged on as team members

3

talked about what they were doing in their departments, information that was largely irrelevant to the majority of the group. As a management team, those people were only loosely coupled and so their meetings should have focused only on issues that cut across departments. Listening to all of those department reports didn't seem productive to them, but they assumed it was what they needed to do to be a real team.

Mistake #2: Picking the right team type but the wrong roles. The human resources department within a West Coast utility company decided to break up the organization's functional silos and create self-directed work teams. So they formed cross-functional teams, putting a person from payroll, benefits, labor relations, and so forth on each team. Then they decided to cross-train everyone on everyone else's job and assign each team member a different client department within the agency. The outcome: If a department's HRD contact used to be a payroll person but there was a labor relations question, the department would get the best information that person could offer—and that wasn't enough!

What the human resource department mistakenly did was design *out* the interdependence, so clients got the best and the worst of their HRD contact instead of the wisdom of the whole team. They also confused knowledge work with physical work. Although manufacturing teams commonly cross-train everyone, that is much less effective in knowledge work. It would have been more successful had they assigned the whole team a set of customers. It's fine to provide an initial point of contact for the clients, but complex issues should come to the whole team so it can examine the synergies among its functions and provide a whole systems response to the need.

Mistake #3: Picking the wrong team type and applying the wrong methods. A team of graphic designers had been formed to make a recommendation to management about the purchase of new computer equipment. The majority of the organization used Windows-based personal computers but the graphic artists were passionate about using the Macintosh platform. The team expended many months in emotional bickering and accomplished nothing. The facilitator used a typical total quality problem-solving process: write a problem statement, analyze the problem, review possible options, and develop a recommendation. But framing the goal of providing a recommendation as a problem only fed the emotional fire: "The problem is that management doesn't listen to us," team members harped. This was not a problem-solving team, however; it was a task force. When the team was presented with a clear description of its purpose, a picture of the comparative analyses it would need to complete, and a schedule, things turned around. After five half-day meetings over a couple of weeks, the team made its recommendations and management accepted them. The success resulted from using the appropriate practices for the team's purpose.

In this chapter, we will explore team types and share best practices for each. First, however, let's examine where teams are needed within an organization and what purposes they serve.

Where Do We Need Teams?

If your organization is interested in implementing a team-based structure, you have recognized that you need to involve many people to get almost anything done these days. The work environment has become so complex that one person rarely can know enough to be able to make a decision alone. Instead, we have to weave together the knowledge of many people. This weaving or integration happens at different levels of an organization (Figure 1.1).

Figure 1.1
Levels of Integration

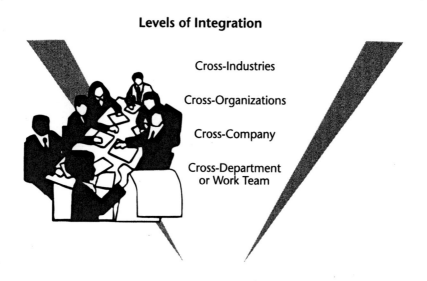

Levels of Integration

Cross-Industries

Cross-Organizations

Cross-Company

Cross-Department
or Work Team

Courtesy of AXIS Performance Advisors and MetaSkills.

At the smallest unit of the organization, we need teams that work within a specific department. For example, in your training department you often need to integrate the knowledge of instructional designers, graphic designers, media specialists, and trainers to produce an effective program. But that is not the only level within the organization that requires teaming. You also need integration across the company. If your training resources are limited, you need a mechanism for deciding what your department will and will not do. Sometimes there are opportunities to combine resources and meet multiple needs.

If your organization is a large one, you also may need to integrate across companies under the same corporate umbrella. In that case, you want to look primarily for synergies. For example, 3-M has done a remarkable job of taking a new technology from one company and creating in many other divisions a chain reaction of new products serving entirely different industry segments. Typically, divisions miss opportunities for synergy but you can gain competitive advantage if you can get them to cooperate.

Probably the most difficult area in which to do teaming, but the one with the greatest potential, is across organizations because that is where major innovations are born. Think about the Internet for a moment. How many industries had to develop and cooperate for the World Wide Web to become a viable industry? The telecommunications industry had to produce fiber optics so we could get fast transmissions; the computer industry had to invent personal computers and make use of an existing mainframe-based network; the software industry had to create graphic interfaces, because we all didn't want to learn UNIX! And those are only some of the contributing factors.

According to Hamel and Prahalad (1994), authors of *Competing for the Future,* becoming a leader in your industry requires that you either

- fundamentally change how business is done in your industry (for example, Charles Schwab Corporation invented discount brokerages)
- redraw the boundaries between industries (for example, Time Warner Inc. pioneered edutainment)
- create entirely new industries (for example, Apple Computer Inc. created the personal computer).

Those strategies usually require innovations in multiple industries. So we need to have teamwork at different levels of the corporation, and each level brings along its own challenges. For example, at the work team level, unclear roles can lead to conflict, and an inability to give honest feedback can inhibit performance. At the broadest level, across industries, culture clashes and misunderstanding the language people use can get in the way of cooperative effort.

What Is the Team's Purpose?

Before you can know how to support a team effort at any level, you must be clear about its purpose. Why do you need a team? What does it need to accomplish to be successful, to add value? There are six basic purposes for teaming:

1. do "work" (produce an item or service)
2. share learning
3. coordinate resources
4. solve problems
5. plan or develop strategies
6. innovate and create.

We can map those purposes to the different organizational levels mentioned above. At a work group level, teams often perform their core work and solve problems. Across a company, one usual key purpose is to plan strategies and coordinate resources. Across industries, the focus is often on innovation. Obviously, each of those purposes would lead the team to operate differently, but most people treat teams as if they were an amorphous mass, indistinguishable from one another. Although there are many well-understood characteristics of success that are true across all team types—open communication, shared goals, and the like—what is less well understood is that each team also has significantly different needs.

Which Team Type Is Appropriate for Your Purpose?

When you looked at the six purposes above, you probably began to map them against the types of teams you have used. For example, self-directed teams are typically used to do the core work in a department. Perhaps you have problem-solving teams or quality improvement teams that generate solutions for identified business problems. You may have a steering committee that develops the implementation plan and coordinates resources for self-directed teams.

Table 1.1 cross-references the purposes to the most common team types, presenting the *primary purpose* of each team. To some degree, all the teams perform other functions. For example, a project team developing a new training program must also develop plans, coordinate resources, and innovate. But its primary purpose is to complete a project—to design and develop a training product for a specific client—and then to disband (or start a new project).

Each team type has different needs and challenges. For example, management teams often have trouble acting as a team at all. One of our clients, a genetic engineering firm whose directors were mostly scientists, was missing most of their customers' delivery dates. Instead of taking joint responsibility for fixing the problem, the management team members pointed fingers: "We're working as hard as we can in my department; the problem must be somewhere else." Project teams may have to integrate core and non-core members. For example, many information technology teams struggle with when to involve the database technicians in an application development project. In contrast, SDWTs rarely have non-core members.

As you consider the team types, it may occur to you that some have very well understood practices. Project teams have project management software, Gantt charts, and critical path analysis, for example. Problem-solving teams have a structured problem-solving process (that is, write a problem statement, brainstorm causes, and so forth) and the total quality tools. Self-directed teams have star points, cross-training, hand-off lists, and work redesign analyses, among other practices. The other team types undoubtedly also have best practices but those are less well understood or standardized. The meetings of each of those team types tend to be significantly different, and you need to know that if you're facilitating them.

As you implement SDWTs, you will probably need many team types. In addition to the self-directed teams themselves, you also may have a management team or representative committee (that is, a steering committee or transition team) that manages the implementation. Their members may charter task forces to redesign such business systems as compensation, performance reviews, and business planning. You will not be implementing only self-directed teams.

Table 1.1
Which Team Do You Need?

Team Type	Purpose					
	Do Work	Share Learning	Coordinate Resources	Solve Problems	Plan/ Develop Strategies	Innovate/ Create
Self-directed work team: inter-dependent members who share the responsibility for completing a whole piece of work and who share leadership, performing most or all the duties of a traditional supervisor	X					
Task force: ad hoc, short-term team formed to solve a particular problem, address an issue, develop a recommendation, design a work process, and so forth					X	X
Problem-solving team: short-term team formed to solve a particular problem (one type of a task force); examples include quality improve-ment teams, process improvement teams, and "green" teams that focus on environmental issues				X		
Project team: team members with complementary skill sets who work on a project with a clear beginning and a clear ending	X					
Product development team: a cross-functional team, sometimes even including customers and vendors, that is responsible for creating new products or services						X
Representative committee: a team whose members sit as representa-tives for others, usually to make decisions or recommendations on behalf of their constituencies				X	X	
Management team: a collection of managers representing inter-dependent functions who must plan and coordinate their efforts				X	X	
Communities of practice: informal groups that come together primarily to learn from each other. Members do similar work but may not be interdependent—they do not require each other in order to do their jobs; instead they mutually benefit by sharing tips, techniques, and the like.	X					

To make matters even more complex, sometimes a team must temporarily mutate from one type to another. Take a self-directed team that has identified a quality problem. The team must know how to switch gears into a problem-solving mode using the tools and practices of a problem-solving team. Once the problem is solved, it switches back to being a self-directed team. Team types are not so much fixed containers as they are sets of practices that serve specific purposes.

There are additional characteristics to consider as you plan to support the various teams in your organization. One factor is the team's duration: whether it is a standing, permanent fixture (for example, a SDWT or a management team) or a temporary one (for example, a task force or project team). Table 1.2 presents a host of variables to consider when forming, training, and supporting teams. As you might imagine, each of those variables raises new issues. Permanent teams may be reluctant to let a member move on, and temporary ones sometimes keep meeting long after their mission is accomplished. Full-time teams are more likely to have personal issues flare up, and part-time teams struggle with multiple priorities. Homogenous teams need to worry about "groupthink," and diverse teams must learn to appreciate and leverage their differences. Co-located teams may become so tight that they create an us–them thinking pattern, whereas virtual or dispersed teams may have trouble maintaining unity. Tightly interdependent teams must closely coordinate their efforts, but loosely coupled teams may not know when to come together. And creative tasks require that people think outside the box, but routine work can lead to boredom.

What Are the Best Practices?

When your organization has determined a team's purpose and picked the best type of team to serve that purpose, then you must use the best practices for that team type. The following is experience-based advice for each team type, and, because of the current interest in virtual (dispersed) teams, there is also some advice about that characteristic in the discussion.

High-Performance or Self-Directed Work Team

To produce the best results, incorporate these practices:

- Hand off leadership responsibilities over time; make clear what responsibilities each person "owns" at a particular time (for example,

Table 1.2
Additional Variables to Consider When Forming and Supporting Teams

Common Characteristics	Team Type							
	Self-Directed Work Team	Task Force	Problem-Solving Team	Project Team	Product Development Team	Representative Committee	Management Committee	Communities of Practice
Duration:								
permanent	X				X	X	X	X
temporary		X	X	X	X	X		
Commitment:								
full-time	X	X		X	X		X	
part-time		X	X	X	X	X	X	X
Composition:								
homogeneous	X		X					X
diverse	X	X	X	X	X	X	X	
Location:								
co-located	X	X	X	X	X	X	X	X
dispersed		X	X	X	X	X	X	X
Interdependence:								
tight	X		X	X	X			
loose		X	X		X	X	X	X
Task:								
creative		X	X	X	X	X	X	X
routine	X					X	X	X

what the manager owns for now and what the team has the power to decide).

• Encourage cross-training to the degree that makes sense. With routine work (for example, manufacturing) cross-train on horizontal tasks, learning one another's jobs. With knowledge work, in which people tend to become specialists, it may not be wise to cross-train. Instead, become sufficiently familiar with one another's work to understand the challenges and interdependencies, but focus on sharing vertical/management tasks instead.

- Make sure the members are technically competent before implementing self-direction.
- Provide a nonthreatening process for evaluating team and individual performance frequently.
- Align organizational systems to encourage teamwork.
- Teach team managers how to coach, facilitate, and support the team without taking over or abdicating their responsibility.
- Keep the team focused on performance, not on members' personal preferences; the team must make decisions in the best interest of the organization.
- Ensure that the natural consequences of the team's work flow back to them directly (for example, customer feedback, rework, and repairs).

Task Force

To produce the best results, incorporate these practices:

- Establish a clear charter or purpose, with clear boundaries.
- Provide tight deadlines and concentrated effort (for example, complete the task in one month, meet two half-days instead of one hour a week).
- Identify a sponsor with clout who can provide resources, guidance, and preselling of recommendations.
- Make clear at the outset what the team can decide and what it can only recommend.
- Give the task force the responsibility for implementing its ideas where possible.

Problem-Solving Team

The following practices will help produce good solutions:

- Provide a systematic problem-solving process that avoids solution jumping (the tendency of people to come up with a solution before thoroughly understanding the problem).

- Establish self-documenting, structured group problem-solving strategies and techniques.
- Provide direct access to anyone with relevant information.
- Offer help in justifying the costs of recommendations and in preparing a presentation to management.
- Let the team present its recommendations so it maintains ownership of them and gets direct feedback.

Project Team

Incorporate these practices to make the most of the project team:

- Use project management methods that are sufficient for the complexity of the project.
- Get customers or clients sufficiently involved to view themselves as part of the team.
- Ensure that project planning involves all core team members so that each one understands the whole project.
- Conduct review meetings at major milestones. Share relevant learning with other project teams.
- Select a project leader/coordinator who keeps an eye on the big picture, resources, deadlines; but make sure all team members are somewhat familiar with one another's roles and responsibilities and feel responsible for the whole project. Sample strategies for prompting joint accountability include having to train customers or users, supporting the software once it's implemented, and earning team bonuses.
- Ensure that auxiliary team members are involved at the outset in planning so that they know well in advance that their assistance will be needed and so that they can shape the project. They should be kept abreast of progress and schedule changes but should attend team meetings only when they have relevant input.
- Connect all team members with their customer (by getting direct feedback and visiting customer sites), but provide the customer with one primary contact person.

Product Development Team

To produce optimal results, incorporate these practices:

- Provide clear goals and criteria for the product or service (for example, cost, features).
- Include on the team representatives of all major stakeholder groups, including people who use, build, repair, and sell the product.
- De-emphasize professional status so that, for example, maintenance technicians feel as free to speak as do engineers. But on any particular issue have the most knowledgeable person make the final decision.
- Consider maintaining the same membership for several product development cycles to leverage the synergy that develops. Change membership when you need to encourage fresh thinking.
- Use nature as a source for creative inspirations.

Representative Committee

To produce the best results, incorporate these practices:

- Make sure you have the right people on the committee so that they can make decisions. Determine what factions need to be represented? Consider people outside your organization, such as customers, vendors, and union officials.
- Where possible, let constituents select their representatives—but provide employees with guidelines for making those selections. The guidelines usually include such suggestions as choose someone you trust and respect, a good communicator, one who is not afraid to speak out, a creative thinker, someone knowledgeable about the faction he or she represents, and someone who does not generate defensive reactions.
- *Involve* constituents rather than merely communicating with them. Don't let the team take on more responsibility than is warranted. Where possible, get the constituents to define priorities and perhaps vote on options. The committee's job is to do the behind-

the-scenes work to come up with viable options. The constituents should feel as if the committee is working for them, not the other way around.

- If the committee has a long life, rotate membership so that you do not create "pseudomanagers," co-workers who are resented for their power and access to leaders. Stagger the rotations to provide an organizational memory and continuity.

- Establish clear authority boundaries. This group should be able to make decisions, not just recommend actions to management. Otherwise, the group is redundant with management and will resent being "overruled."

- When a decision is made, take time to explain why it was made (especially if it is not a popular decision). Explain it, explain it, and explain it again. Be absolutely truthful.

- Make most of your meetings public. Encourage others to sit in. Invite specific people. Post the agenda in advance, and leave room on the sheet for people to make notes. Communicate the outcomes of meetings in several ways.

Management Team

The following practices will yield good results for a management team:

- Clarify the purpose of the team. Is it to coordinate resources, set goals, make decisions that affect all members' departments, or just to learn from one another?

- Make sure the managers feel jointly accountable for their task. That may include having a portion of their individual compensation based on the performance of each other's areas.

- Break down turf boundaries or fiefdoms through dialogue, cross-training, joint responsibilities, job rotation, and so forth.

- Explore the team members' interdependencies and shared needs. Many managers feel very isolated and independent from one another, and often they can benefit immensely from mutual support.

- Use team-building activities to develop trust and openness, but make sure the managers see a direct link between those activities and the work they must do.

Communities of Practice (Learning Teams)

Informal groups can benefit when you integrate the following practices:

- Permit casual mingling and sharing.
- Encourage people to share their cheat-sheets and other unofficial tools they have developed.
- Avoid formalizing these groups; the need to communicate should drive the desire.
- Organize the physical space to encourage informal communication sharing. For example, place whiteboards near the coffee machine and flipcharts in the cafeteria.
- If the team feels it's appropriate, help it build tools or databases—but only if the team is convinced it will keep them updated and use them.
- Help everyone notice the things they've learned or things they know that are worth sharing. People often discount their own knowledge.

Virtual (Dispersed) Teams

When starting virtual teams, integrate the following practices:

- If people are not co-located, it may be easier to define clearly separate roles. Think subassembly—discrete components that can be combined easily. Only form a virtual team if you need the creativity or pooled knowledge it provides.
- Establish a standard, proven process to launch new teams, tailored to the degree of interdependency required. Agree on the meanings of important words. Develop special ground rules for working at a distance (for example, how to communicate important information, how often to check email, and how to resolve conflicts).
- First, give the team time to develop a relationship face-to-face; it is easier to *maintain* a relationship from a distance than it is to create one.

The following practices will help to sustain virtual teams:

- Make all information available to every member. Virtual teams need virtual information. Use local-area networks, groupware, videoconferencing, and shared databases. Build a culture of trust, openness, and honored commitments. Make information hoarding a career-limiting behavior.

- Provide training on how to facilitate teleconferences and videoconferences because those are more difficult than face-to-face meetings. Establish a schedule for meetings so everyone can plan to participate. If members speak different languages, encourage people to express emotional issues in their native tongue before translating their comments into the shared language; that serves as a means of communicating the tone of the message. Also, if members are globally dispersed, vary the times when conferences are held so the burden of meeting at odd hours is shared.

- Periodically meet face-to-face to resolve issues and deepen relationships. Twice a year is a good guideline. The travel costs should pay off in improved performance.

When disbanding virtual teams, consider these practices:

- Make sure everyone wins. If everyone leaves a virtual team better able to contribute to the next, such teams will be sustainable.

- Have an ending ceremony, celebration, or learning event to help participants let go and move forward. Virtual teams need closure if the members are to reform as other groups.

- Facilitate ongoing relationships where appropriate. Feed employees' social needs by building an enduring network. For example, at all-employee events provide time for virtual team members to reconnect.

About the Author

Darcy Hitchcock, president of Axis Performance Advisors, is recognized as an expert in the implementation of collaborative business systems, including high-performance work teams. Among her published articles and books are *Why TQM Fails and What to Do About It* (1994, Irwin);

Why Teams Fail and What to Do About It (1995, Irwin); and *The Work Redesign Team Handbook: A Step-by-Step Guide for Creating Self-Directed Teams* (1994, Quality Resources). Hitchcock is a popular presenter at international conferences. As an advocate for socially responsible business practices, she sits on the board of Business for Social Responsibility.

The goal is to make money for the company.
Putting people together is only the beginning;
staying together is a challenge; working
together is success.

— Ed Rose

Chapter 2

What Is a Self-Directed Work Team?

William A. Levinson

A self-directed work team[1] combines the best aspects of the independent craft worker with mass production. It integrates the craft worker's intimate knowledge of the task with all the advantages of standardization. It provides an organizational structure that puts the employees in control of achieving their goals.

Predators, Prey, and Autonomous Work Groups

Tyrannosaurus rex was a terrifying predator with a huge appetite and a brain about the size of a walnut. If something happened at the *T. rex's* tail, it took a while for the information to reach the brain. The brain had to think about what to do, and then send the instructions to do it. By that time, the situation had probably changed. "Where did my dinner go? Who stole my egg?" That is a good description of a traditional (Taylor) management system (see the *"Taylorsaurus rex"* in Figure 2.1). Taylorism, a management model whose extreme form views workers as robots, tells the frontline workers—the organization's arms and legs—to leave their brains at the factory gate. Management does the thinking and planning, and frontline workers follow instructions. It often takes a long time for information to flow from the front line to management, and then back. Most trainers are familiar with that model and the effect it has had on organizations in the twentieth century. I believe that Taylor's approach was very effective in its time, given the developmental phase of the Industrial Age, and I believe it safe to say that Taylor's approach was the one used in most factories until the late 1980s.

The tyrannosaurus was dominant when its competitors were other dinosaurs but it could not compete with mammals. A fast, agile, relatively large-brained, warm-blooded mammal could grab a tyrannosaurus egg and run before the big dinosaur could react. A scavenger mammal could steal part of the tyrannosaurus's dinner. Today, small, innovative, and

Figure 2.1
Taylorsaurus Rex

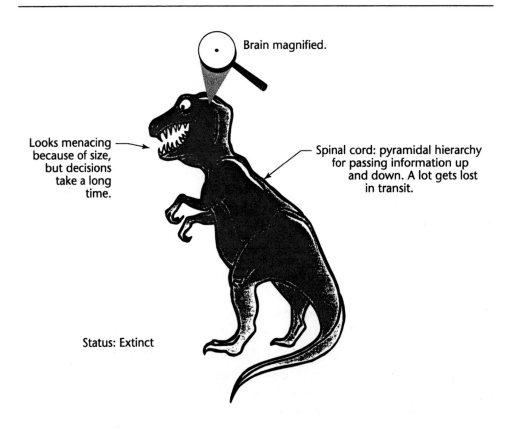

Brain magnified.

Looks menacing because of size, but decisions take a long time.

Spinal cord: pyramidal hierarchy for passing information up and down. A lot gets lost in transit.

Status: Extinct

adaptable companies can steal pieces of their big competitors' market shares. Successful competitors customize their products and services for individual customers, and small, independent teams do this best.

In the Information Age (with the global marketplace that it created), the traditional approach to running a factory or any other organization cannot continue to work for long. Organizations must use fully their most valuable resources—their employees. The traditional management model is much like the tyrannosaurus—if it doesn't change it will become extinct. Today, companies must have different organizational structures filled with different kinds of workers. They can deploy teams and be equally competitive in a world that demands the lowest cost, the highest quality, on-time delivery, and world-class service.

Milliken & Co.'s Customer Action Teams and Harris Semiconductor's Customer Contact Teams are examples. Progressive organizations are changing their traditional management structures in favor of a team-based culture. In that team-based culture, the workers strive toward a shared goal. They believe their work has value to others and they have team and organizational values that guide their day-to-day job decisions. The organization provides them with a structure that puts them in control of achieving their goals—some refer to that structure as SDWTs. That type of organizational structure is very similar to the Lernian Hydra, a nine-headed serpent in Greek mythology. If something happened near one head, it did not have to wait for instructions. That head could think independently and react to the danger or opportunity. That is a good description of an organic, adaptive organization, and each head is like a self-directed work team. Unlike the organizational dinosaur, the organic system delegates the decision process to the front line. The thinking and the follow-up action occur at the scene of the critical activity, thus enabling employees to be in control of achieving their own goals.

Progressive managers recognize that the person who is closest to the job knows more about it than anyone else. They establish organizational structures like SDWTs to facilitate decision making at the lowest level possible.

SDWTs and Principle-Centered Leadership

The SDWT is a natural element of a principle-centered organization. Stephen Covey (1991) wrote that organizational principles are like a compass. A map (that is, a "traditional organization's" operating procedures and rules) is useful only in a static, well-known environment. It is of little value in a dynamic environment or in new territory. The compass, *or shared principles and vision,* will work anywhere. Self-directed workers use this compass, plus empowering work skills, to adapt to rapid change and new competitive challenges.

There is a direct tie-in to the role of the frontline worker. "The people who are closest to the action in the wilderness can use that compass and their own expertise and judgment to make decisions and take actions. . . . If you focus on principles, you empower everyone who understands those principles to act without constant monitoring, evaluating, correcting, or controlling" (Covey, 1991, p. 98). That means that frontline workers must understand the organization's principles, values, and goals, and have the training and autonomy to support them. It is critical that HRD trainers understand that strategy.

In a traditional, rule-centered organization, the frontline worker must often consult the rule book or ask for direction. Why is that wrong? Suppose the activity is a service desk, and there are people waiting. If the employee has to consult the manager frequently, the internal and external customers will become frustrated. In a traditional organization, assembly workers may have to wait an hour or more for a technician to fix a problem. If the workers can fix the problem themselves, they can save valuable production time. "Empowerment" requires that workers have both the competence (training) and the authority to act without waiting for direction. They view their work as being worthwhile, in their control, and having the respect of the organization. That is a simple concept, but there is a large investment required by management to make the transition from a traditional to a self-directed organization.

When we first started the process of changing to a self-directed structure at Harris Semiconductor (now known as Intersil Corporation), it was almost like upper management sprinkled pixie dust over the organization and said, "Go forth—now you are Empowered." It didn't work. Organizations must commit to a significant investment in training, and HRD trainers must be willing and able to facilitate the process. This book will provide you with guidance, along with some tools to assist you in the transformation. It will include information that you can share with management on SDWT history, case studies, and the pitfalls and weaknesses that you are likely to encounter during the transition.

Self-Direction and Autonomy: Some History

It is very instructive and often fascinating to look at historical precedents to modern management techniques. Self-direction and worker empowerment are not new concepts. Consider the trade system that existed for hundreds of years. The average shop was under the direction of a master tradesperson, who was also the owner. The master often supervised journeymen and apprentices who did not schedule or direct their own work but who could progress to higher levels by displaying proficiency. Apprentices usually graduated to journeyman status, which meant that they could perform many shop tasks independently. A proficient journeyman could become a master, open a shop, and train others. The system, however, did not involve autonomous work groups.

Japanese Work Groups

The cohesiveness of Japanese work groups may be a product of Japanese history. In coastal fishing villages, people had to work together to succeed. Families learned to depend on each other, and this carried over into modern Japanese culture where teaming seems to come naturally, often without any formal authority figure. That is why the teaming structure is so successful in Japanese factories. There are also some theorists who believe that the Japanese modeled their industries after an aristocratic society in which peasants provided their labor to the local lord and received land to work, protection, and shelter in return. When Japanese industrialists realized that industrialization was the key to power, they simply grafted industrial systems onto their autocratic system. Symbolically, the *shoguns* and *samurai* became the industrial managers, providing for the needs of the workers. The concept of "lifetime employment" was merely the old system expressed in the new terms of the Industrial Age.

Work Groups in American History

In contrast to the Japanese model, American history accounts for our ideal of self-sufficiency. In contemporary popular American culture, movies stress the "rugged individualist." This ideal comes from our frontier and pioneering heritage. Frontier families often lived miles from each other. Individualism and the ability to handle one's own problems were desirable qualities. That does not mean that people were loathe to help each other. In rural and frontier regions of the United States, passersby were more likely to help a stranded traveler or intervene to stop a crime. Unlike city dwellers, they could not count on police or other emergency assistance being nearby. If someone's ranch was under attack by bandits or desperados, the neighbors would band together to help—if for no other reason than fear that they'd be next if they didn't act to stop the problem. However, the people did not work together in the same way that Japanese fishermen did. American industry tended to follow the military model for managing employees, using a "chain of command" approach to communication and other activities.

Amish Work Groups and Barn Construction

The Amish are a religious sect that originated in Germany and settled in a number of rural areas of the United States. Most Amish choose not to own machinery or electrical appliances, and they rely on animal-powered farm equipment. When an Amish family needs a new barn, their neighbors gather for a "barn-raising" at which everybody helps to construct the new building. Any supervision is of the informal kind, so this is an excellent example of a true self-directed group. The participants have the empowering skills, like carpentry and knowledge of farms, that enable them to cooperate naturally and smoothly. They share what they learn with each other. From my years spent in Pennsylvania living around Amish communities, I have found their cooperative endeavors to be made possible by their cultural behaviors—good listening skills, creativity, a positive outlook, and respect for other people and their ideas, even when they do not agree with them. Those behaviors are a good foundation for teamwork of any kind. The Amish provide a good example of just how valuable effective team behaviors are to the success of a group.

Self-Directed Coal Miners in England

Self-directed coal mining teams developed as long ago as the 1860s. They evolved not by deliberate design but by the nature of the job. Miners used "hand-got methods" of getting coal from short coal faces. They worked in groups of three men: a hewer, his mate, and an assistant called a "trammer." The three men formed a cohesive group that handled a complete cycle of coal-getting operations. The miners took pride in their craft and operated independently in the mines because supervision was impossible. The men in those small groups chose each other, helped each other, and built enduring relationships. Those relationships went beyond work, and included caring for each other's families when there was sickness or an accident. Whatever the conditions for mining, the miners knew that they could depend on one another. Again, a key ingredient for success in these teams was the effective interpersonal behaviors of their members.

The introduction of the longwall mining method was psychologically devastating to the miners. When mechanization was introduced, long walls for coal gathering were substituted for short faces. Machines did the work of the small groups. The complete cycle of coal getting took place over three shifts. The new method isolated the miners from each other and destroyed the camaraderie of the face-to-face group. The results of the longwall method were lower productivity, tension, and anxiety for the miners. Although the longwall method was more amenable to mechanization, it hurt morale—the miners could no longer interact with one another on such a personal level. That result prompted study of the social and psychological conditions of coal miners which showed that hand-got mining was clearly better for morale and motivation.

Socio-Technical Systems Theory

The Tavistock Institute of Human Relations in London helped formulate what is now called socio-technical systems theory (STS). The research of Trist and Bamforth contributed to the self-directed team model. According to STS theory, organizational productivity depends on technological and social elements. When planning a new work structure, managers must consider the task requirements of the job and the employee's social and psychological needs. If all of those needs are not considered in the new design, both productivity and morale will suffer. The SDWT work design supports and exemplifies STS theory.

Self-Directed Teams at General Motors

Peters (1987) described the empowerment of workers at the Delco Remy plant in Fitzgerald, Georgia. Workers there are responsible for

1. all quality control, with support available from experts *when necessary*
2. all maintenance and minor repairs
3. housekeeping and safety
4. budgeting (capital and operating)
5. staffing, recruiting, and layoffs. For example, instead of laying people off, everybody may work fewer hours.

The workers also are given access to personal improvement tools and educational opportunities, and they are paid for learning new skills (a "pay-for-knowledge" program).

Workstation Ownership at International Business Machines Corporation

IBM's plant at East Fishkill, New York, introduced a workstation ownership program in the late 1980s. Workstation ownership is similar to the craftworker's responsibility for a complete task. Under the program, operators take responsibility for production, quality, and maintenance. The program also encourages operators to improve quality and productivity. To empower the operators, IBM put them through almost two years of community college classes. The workers learned math, physics, chemistry, electronics, and statistical process control (SPC). When they had completed those courses successfully, they needed just a few more courses to qualify for an associate's degree (Levinson, 1994).

Self-Directed Work Teams Defined

A self-directed work team is a small group of people empowered to manage themselves and their daily work. Such teams are formal, permanent organizational units. Team members typically not only handle their current job responsibilities, but also plan and schedule their work, manage production, solve problems, and share leadership responsibilities. The empowerment relies on the following three assumptions:

1. Those closest to the work know more about it than does anyone else and know best how to perform and improve their job.
2. Most employees want to "own" their jobs and contribute to the effectiveness of their organization.

3. Teams provide opportunities for empowerment that are not available to individual employees.

What Do Self-Directed Work Teams Do?

A self-directed work team usually performs many traditional support functions along with routine production or service. For example, they keep records; select, orient, and train new members; keep attendance records; control quality; plan work schedules; resolve conflicts; assign jobs; monitor performance; solve technical problems; discipline members; control absences and tardiness; order materials and supplies; prepare budgets; and control inventory.

SDWTs exhibit the following characteristics:

- The team performs specific tasks.
- Team members are multiskilled.
- Team members are interdependent.
- Team members are in control of their daily, monthly, and yearly goals.
- The team's focus is on team results, not individual results.
- Team members rotate tasks because extensive cross-training enables them to perform many different jobs.
- Management clearly defines the team's boundaries for task responsibilities and authority (for example, hiring or firing members, or redefining work instructions, may be outside of the team's authority).
- The team monitors and controls both its work quantity and quality.
- Each team understands the need for effective teaming behaviors.

Do Self-Directed Work Teams Really Work?

The answer is a qualified "yes." There have been some failures. SDWTs have a long history, although they have existed under many different names. The idea behind all of them is the same: Give employees many of the responsibilities normally carried out by supervisors. Self-directed teams work best where there is management support and ongoing training. There also must be a transition period for transfer of supervisory responsibilities to the work group.

Johnsonville Sausage provides a dramatic example of SDWT's success. The expectation of hourly workers there fits the stereotype of workers in a Tayloristic system: "Leave your brains at the factory gate and make sausages." But at Johnsonville SDWTs actually performed the following tasks (Peters, 1989):

- developed and tracked annual budgets
- developed proposals for capital investments
- took full responsibility for quality control
- monitored and improved productivity and quality
- developed new products and new packaging.

That is not what one expects from hourly workers who often have no more than high school diplomas, but motivated workers often exceed management's expectations. If managers expect them to behave like pairs of hands that only take direction, that is what will happen. If managers motivate and empower them to use their judgment and experience and to contribute their ideas and expertise, they will. *Expectations about behavior are often self-fulfilling.*

Many major organizations have implemented self-directed teams, including General Motors, Procter & Gamble, Ford Motor Company, Digital Equipment Corp., Volvo, Xerox Corp., Shenandoah Life Insurance Co., AT&T Corp., Bell Laboratories, American Transtech, Yale University Library, Sherwin-Williams Co., Employees' Aid Association for Lutherans, Honeywell Inc., and Monsanto Co. The list is long and will lengthen. The critical issue is how an organization manages the installation process. Some organizations do it carefully and effectively; others expect self-management to occur magically. Organizations hoping for instant, magical success will be disappointed.

The contributors to this book believe that SDWTs provide a competitive edge by empowering employees to practice continuous improvement through their taking ownership of their work cell. The transition to an empowered workforce is a process, not an event. The process must be supported by strategic training initiatives that focus on the organization's objectives. A SDWT structure requires new resources and changes in the way we conduct our business. With management support, the training professional becomes the champion of the process.

Characteristics of Self-Directed Work Teams

In choosing what to call these empowered teams (for example, self-directed or high-performance), the key is deciding as an organization what the vision of these teams is, communicating that vision to the teams, and then calling them whatever you like. I believe that as long as you have consistency throughout the organization, the name doesn't matter. The definition, and therein the name, of these teams can vary within an organization as long as the vision is clear and constant. For example, Harris Semiconductor's Palm Bay, Florida, plant defines self-managed work teams as "small groups of people empowered to manage themselves and the work they do on a day-to-day basis—performing 85 percent to 90 percent of their daily work without outside resources." Steve Gilmore and Ed Rose formulated this definition in 1990 to help the Palm Bay (non-union) site set a direction for development.

The staff management team at Harris's Mountaintop, Pennsylvania, (union) plant, however, defines SDWTs in the following words:

> Self-directed work teams are natural work groups. Each SDWT is responsible for a business process that delivers a product or service to an internal or external customer. Each SDWT manages its business within defined boundary conditions. Its continued improvements for the success of the business are the measurement of its performance. (Wentz, 1998, p. 59)

If you study those two definitions closely, you will see that they are not very different. Exhibit 2.1 presents the charter and code of conduct from a team organized to improve product quality. I share those examples only to make the point about naming and defining; neither is meant to be a universal definition of SDWTs. The definition will change based on your work environment and existing boundaries within your organization. Throughout the book, I and the other contributors will offer examples from our own experience at Harris. We include them only to show what *we* have done. In some cases, those examples will be variations of what

Exhibit 2.1
Team Charter and Code of Conduct

Purpose

The goal of the Crazy 8 team is to implant ("implant" refers to ion implantation, a process for treating silicon semiconductor discs) every wafer (disc) accurately and as quickly as possible for our customers. We will work continuously to reduce costs and improve wafer yields.

The Crazy 8 team will be contributing to Mountaintop and Harris Corporation, setting new standards for tomorrow's semiconductors.

Code of Conduct

1. Give everyone an opportunity to speak.
2. Listen carefully to the ideas and contributions of other members.
3. All members of the team should make an individual effort to support the team decisions.
4. Carry out team assignments on schedule.
5. The team meeting is confidential ("what is said here, stays here").
6. Team members should not avoid conflict, but address it and resolve it in a respectful and professional manner.
7. Team members should bring things up in meetings, not after leaving the meeting.

you have done and seen before. For others, they may provide a place to start the transition. Either way, they are provided as a sort of benchmark in the process of transitioning to SDWT.

Star Organization

In 1996, Harris's Mountaintop plant introduced the *star organization* for its SDWTs. Harris's plant in Palm Bay has been using the star organization since about 1989. It is an improvement over the SDWT with a single team leader—instead of assigning all the work to one person, it distributes it among several people. It is actually similar to a professional

Figure 2.2
Star Organization

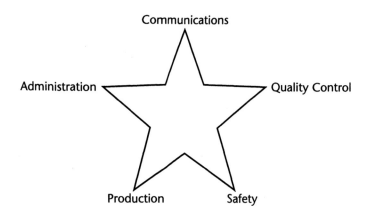

or civic organization, which has a president, newsletter editor, treasurer, activities coordinator, and so on. The system assigns a person to perform each critical task, thereby avoiding the problem, "If everybody is responsible, nobody is responsible" (Levinson and Tumbelty, 1997). Figure 2.2 depicts a star organization with five coordinators, although a star can have any number of points.

Exhibit 2.2 links the five points of that star organization to the work of the team chartered by Exhibit 2.1, the Crazy 8 Ion Implantation Team, and enumerates the tasks assigned to each star-point coordinator.

Exhibit 2.2
Star Points Tasks, Crazy 8 Ion Implantation Team

Administration coordinator:

- keeps a record or calendar of coverage for time off.
- takes meeting minutes and makes them available for absent members and manufacturing leaders.
- manages team projects.

(continued on next page)

Exhibit 2.2
Star Points Tasks, Crazy 8 Ion Implantation Team *(continued)*

- distributes certification training forms, making sure that there are copies available and that everyone knows how to fill them out and where to turn them in.
- organizes training information.

- organizes team meetings (reserves the room; notifies the team leaders, mentor, and facilitator; prepares the agenda).

Communication coordinator:

- facilitates general communications among team members, other shifts, customers, manufacturing leader, engineers, mentors, and facilitator.
- reads team email and makes sure that other team members are aware of its contents.
- orients new employees (introduces new members to the team; shows them evacuation routes, team charter, code of conduct, and so forth).
- acts as social coordinator (provides snacks for meetings, team parties).
- updates general information books.

Production coordinator:

- knows the priority work for production planning and for proper machine staffing.
- monitors constraints and planning to be sure the workload is full.
- monitors hold/static lots.

Safety coordinator:

- observes general safety concerns.
- knows safety contacts (who to approach with safety questions or concerns).
- conducts safety training.
- coordinates facilities request (knows who to contact in case a light goes out and so on).
- updates material safety data sheet.

Endnotes

1. Also known as a high-performance work team.
2. Ford Motor Company's Team-Oriented Problem Solving, Eight Disciplines (TOPS-8D).

About the Author

William A. Levinson is a staff engineer at Harris Semiconductor's site in Mountaintop, Pennsylvania. He holds a bachelor's degree from Pennsylvania State University, a master's in chemical engineering from Cornell University, and a master's of business administration and a master's of science in applied statistics from Union College. He is a registered professional engineer in Pennsylvania, and he holds American Society for Quality (ASQ) certifications in quality engineering, quality management, quality auditing, and reliability engineering. He is the author of *The Way of Strategy* (1994, ASQC Quality Press), co-author of *SPC Essentials and Productivity Improvement: A Manufacturing Approach* (1997, ASQC Quality Press), and editor of *Leading the Way to Competitive Excellence: The Harris Mountaintop Case Study* (1998, ASQC Quality Press).

> Change is an ingredient inherent in organizational life. In successful organizations, change begins with you.
> — Ed Rose

Chapter 3

The Need to Change for Survival and Success

Ed Rose and Steve Buckley

Before an organization can transform itself, it must recognize the need to do so. That sounds straightforward, but failure to recognize the need for change is among the most common barriers to a company's adapting to the new requirements of a global marketplace. "We've always done it this way." "It has always worked before." "If it ain't broke, don't fix it." Those attitudes are roadblocks on the way to SDWTs. Management commitment of resources is critical to the success of any organizational transformation of this magnitude. This chapter and the next will provide trainers with a proven approach to implementing organizational change, and with ideas for presenting and selling their recommendations to management.

Rapid Change: Embrace It or Perish

Tom Peters (1987) wrote, "Violent and accelerating change, now commonplace, will become the grist of the opportunistic winner's mill. The losers will view such confusion as a 'problem' to be 'dealt' with" (p. 14). The competitive environment in the new millennium will be even more turbulent and dynamic than the preceding decades, and the rate of change will only accelerate. Traditional management structures cannot adapt to that environment quickly enough to survive and thrive. The dogmatic Taylor management model that told frontline workers, "Leave your brains at the factory gate" worked in the relatively static environment of the late nineteenth and early twentieth centuries when technological change was much slower and nothing could happen very quickly. It does not work now.

Today's competitive environment does not forgive errors or missed opportunities. The Internet allows small companies and even individuals to offer goods and services internationally. It's possible for a company to have an apparent monopoly one day, and find a competitor from India, Australia, or Denmark eroding the ground beneath them the next. Internet connectivity is available today via television to people without PCs, and it will change the way the general public gets and uses information.

Here is an astounding example of change.[1] The MITS Altair 8800 personal computer appeared on the cover of *Popular Electronics* in January of 1975, and Bill Gates and Paul Allen began writing software for it. They named their company "Microsoft." In 1975, Microsoft had three employees and total revenues of $16,005. Within a decade, PCs were doing to IBM's mainframe market what the private automobile had done to the railroads. By 1998, Microsoft Corporation had grown to 27,320 employees with revenues of $14,480,000,000, and Bill Gates was the richest person in the world.

SDWTs and the Tactical Value of Speed

Speed is vital for survival and success. Empowering people to make decisions at the lowest level possible equals speed. The Russian field marshal Alexander Suvorov (1729–1800) was among the first to apply this principle. Most commanders of his era used large, stately, and ponderous formations to achieve good *centralized control*. "Centralized control" should sound familiar; it is the essence of the mechanistic (Tayloristic) organization. Those commanders wanted the same control over their soldiers that a chess player has over his or her pieces. Battles were often indecisive because no one could do anything very rapidly or unexpectedly.

As long as everybody was "playing chess," no one could achieve a decisive advantage. Suvorov, on the other hand, operated what we might call "empowered fighting units" (the SDWT concept). He decentralized the command and control structure and extensively trained his troops. As a result, he never lost a battle. Decision making *can* equal speed.

SDWTs promote a business culture that can adapt quickly and react wisely to a turbulent environment. Those natural work groups can accept responsibility for the technical, social, and administrative aspects of their work. They develop clear visions of their organizational roles, and that enables them to direct themselves. After receiving the proper training, they do not have to wait for detailed instructions; they can use their collective knowledge, judgment, and initiative.

Organizational Resistance

SDWTs are not commodities an organization can buy off the shelf, like a computer or a manufacturing tool. We must create and develop them, and this requires a substantial managerial commitment of resources, time, and training effort. We must follow Stephen Covey's (1991) Law of the Farm: plow and sow in the spring, nurture the crops during the summer, and harvest in the fall. Hoping to purchase a quick solution off the shelf is like expecting to harvest without plowing or planting.

Traditional managers most likely will question the benefits of investing the necessary money, time, and effort. As the champion of the process, you must ask them if they have considered the long-term results of *not* investing. The choice to remain an organizational dinosaur in the Information Age is not conducive to a company's survival or prosperity.

Managers must develop a clear vision of where they want to lead their organizations, and a plan for accomplishing it. The first step is to break with old, self-limiting paradigms. Those preconceived ways of looking at the world are major barriers to performance. When we tell ourselves, "We can't do it" or "It won't work," then we *can't* do it and it *won't* work (Levinson and Lauffer, 1998). The problem is not a physical, organizational, or social obstacle; it is our attitude.

Lasting change requires adjustment of the organization's culture— changes to its shared expectations, values, and beliefs. Marvin Bower, managing director of the management consulting firm McKinsey & Company, defined culture as "the way we do things around here" (Deal and Kennedy, 1982). A company's culture is its organizational soul.

Keeping the Faith: A Crucial Management Tool

The change process can be very frustrating to managers who have operated under the traditional management model. I have encountered managers saying things like, "Team name? I will give them a name—they don't need to use valuable production time deciding on a name." To some extent, I experienced thoughts like that myself when I was starting out with teams. I never really appreciated the value of naming a team. But little things, like a new identity for a team to relate to, can make a big difference to team development in your organization.

Here's a story that captures the need for managers to have faith in the change process. A man was following his path in life when he came to the shore of a large body of water which he would have to cross, even though he could not swim. A man standing nearby (known to many in the area as a sage) said he could help the man get across the body of water. He requested that the man provide him with a handkerchief and a bill of large denomination. The man knew he had to cross the water to complete his journey, so he gave the sage his handkerchief and the largest bill he had. The sage wrote a magic word on the bill, folded it, wrapped it in the handkerchief, and handed it back to him. The magic word, he was told, would enable him to swim. The man believed what the sage had told him. He walked happily into the water holding the handkerchief, found himself to be floating, and proceeded to swim away from the shore. The sage's process seemed to be working. Halfway across the lake, swimming over many fathoms, the man became curious as to the nature of the magic word he had seen the sage write on the bill. Floating on his back, full of confidence, he unwrapped the handkerchief. There was no magic word and no bill. Feeling betrayed, the man lost faith and sank.

Just like most of us faced with the challenge of implementing teams, the man in that story needed to get from one place to another—across a perilous expanse. Like management, unfamiliar with the process of teaming, the man couldn't swim. He entered the unknown on the strength of someone's assurances but then lost faith—a critical error that managers must not make. They must embrace and sustain faith in the change process they have established and in their employees—even to the point of letting teams expend time deciding on a name for themselves.

Organizational change requires the effective use of benchmarking, consultants, and other forms of information gathering, combined with a strategic approach to implementation. And you must have faith that you are moving in the right direction. That faith, or course, must be connected to a strong vision in order to develop SDWTs that will promote organizational learning.

Organizational Learning: Standardizing Best Practices

We define *organizational learning* in the following terms: The process of the organization identifying its best practices and work standards, and then standardizing those practices and standards for the benefit of the entire organization. Managers should seek the best practices within their areas and identify them for others. Flexibility and speedy response are the primary characteristics of a learning organization, with the organization learning from its mistakes and correcting them systematically.

It is clear to many organizations in the United States and in many other countries around the world that new organizational structures are required. The number of companies turning to team structures is growing rapidly. With today's emphasis on information and the global marketplace, organizations that will succeed must adopt those new organizational structures and may have to break away from products and processes that contributed to past successes. Organizations must have a mechanism in place that allows employees to make decisions that traditionally were reserved for managers. They need to create innovative products and services as well as new techniques and methods for producing and distributing them. The new organizations also will have to take leaps of faith, develop creative solutions to old problems, and learn from their mistakes. If implemented with a structured approach focusing on developing an organizational learning environment, SDWTs will provide the necessary mechanism.

The SDWT organizational structure can form the foundation you need to build a world-class learning organization. Develop a vision of the team structure you want to create in your organization, have faith, follow your instincts, and you will succeed.

Endnote

1. The data referenced come from the Microsoft Museum Website timeline—http://www.microsoft.com/MSCorp/Museum/timelines/microsoft/timeline.asp.

Respect people for who they are.
Nurture their natural abilities.
Don't be surprised when they go beyond
your greatest expectations.

— Ed Rose

Chapter 4

Cultural Transformation: Moving to a Team-Based Culture

Ed Rose and Steve Buckley

To develop strategies for cultural transformation, we must understand the conflict between an organization's need for change and individuals' need for security. Throughout history, people have resisted change because they perceived it as a threat and did not recognize its benefits. For example, the Luddites smashed weaving machinery because they thought it would take away their jobs. They did not recognize that machinery made workers more productive and that enabled employers to pay higher wages. Today, people resist the self-directed work team idea because they perceive it as a threat. Supervisors often must accept non-supervisory roles, and some view that as demotion. Frontline workers who have taken direction for years may feel uncomfortable when given extra responsibility. The management team must lead people through the change process and help them overcome their fears.

41

Change Management

Forces That Promote Change

Organizational change occurs only when the forces that promote it overcome those that resist it. People must recognize the need for change before they will accept it. Some forces that promote organizational change are

- competitive pressures
- legal and economic considerations, such as environmental and workplace regulations
- changing consumer desires and values
- cultural changes
- technological innovation, advances in telecommunications, and exponential growth in knowledge.

Forces That Resist Change

When we think of forces that resist change, we think of organizational inertia. People do not recognize the *need* for change, so they don't do it. There are, however, forces that actively oppose change in most organizations. The following are some examples:

- fear of the unknown
- social norms and expectations
- vested interests in the status quo
- group cohesiveness
- status uncertainty
- ingrained habits
- perception of threats to one's career.

How Change Affects People

An organization's need for change often conflicts with its members' need to maintain their sense of personal security, and change agents must recognize this. When a change is first introduced, what is our first instinctive reaction? It is survival, or how the change will affect us. When implementing any changes in an organization, change agents must be aware of the effects of this natural conflict: the need for the organization to change in order to survive and the need for the employee to maintain his or her sense of personal security. Balancing the conflicting interests may seem like an impossible task, but it is really quite simple if a carefully planned process is followed to manage the change.

Organizations are generally very diligent about managing technological change. Operating manuals and training sessions focus on the physical aspects of the change, and they are both routine and rigorous. Companies, however, do not pay as much attention to the psychological and social impacts of organizational change.

Psychological considerations include those that affect the way people relate to and feel about their jobs. Any change will create doubts and questions in a person's mind. The severity of those doubts depends partially on an individual's personality and experience. Many concerns, however, are predictable. Social considerations include changes in the individual's relationships with others in the work group and with the whole organization. Concerns include alienation from fellow employees, less access to information, and status in a new peer group.

Change agents focus a lot of attention on the behavioral effects of change, but psychological and social aspects are more important. Psychological and social effects prompt predictable questions from the people affected. As a change agent, you can and should anticipate the questions that will arise from the change being implemented. The key lies in placing yourself in the position of those whom the change affects.

Considerations in Introducing Change

Change agents cannot control people's attitudes toward change, their levels of personal security, and the established organizational culture. They can and must, however, control how the change takes place (the rate of change). They must adapt their approach to an employee's current attitudes and to historical events, and they must work within the organizational culture's framework. The organizational culture includes shared expectations about "the way we do things around here." Most people will resist anything that goes against the culture, so change agents must understand the existing culture as much as possible. They must provide the organization with a clear sense of future direction.

Organizational cultures change slowly, but they will respond to successful change management. The facilitator should emphasize any small successes to the organization. A series of small successes, even in a change-resistant culture, will make people more receptive to greater efforts and reduce future resistance to change. Ultimately, the culture may welcome and embrace change as a competitive advantage. Change and innovation will replace inertia and stagnation as "the way we do things around here." An environment of support and encouragement needs to be established, with rewards systems to recognize the new behaviors required. Don't wait until your rewards system is fully agreed to and in place to implement SDWTs.

Training professionals are critical to the success of every aspect of the change process. They must provide the required training for their organization on a just-in-time basis, and form strategic partnerships with the production department, unions, managers, and so forth.

Case Study: Harris's Four-Step Process for Managing Cultural Transformation

To transform their organizational culture, Harris Semiconductor's plant in Palm Bay, Florida, used the process described below. The management team, facilitated by training professionals, defined and integrated a team development process with a four-step change management strategy (Figure 4.1). That combination helped reduce the potential negative effects of the transformation and promoted successful change to self-directed work teams.

Step 1: Recognize the Effect of the Rate of Change on Personal Security

Once you have assessed the organization's need for change and its readiness to undertake it, management must consider the scope of the change and its pace. How receptive is the organization's culture, and what are employees' attitudes toward change? Change management techniques that work well in one culture may fail badly in another.[1] To succeed, change agents must balance the concerns of those whom the change affects with the organization's needs.

In 1980, Harris Semiconductor's top managers realized that the organization had to change to meet competitive challenges. The company

Figure 4.1
Four Steps to Successful Transformations

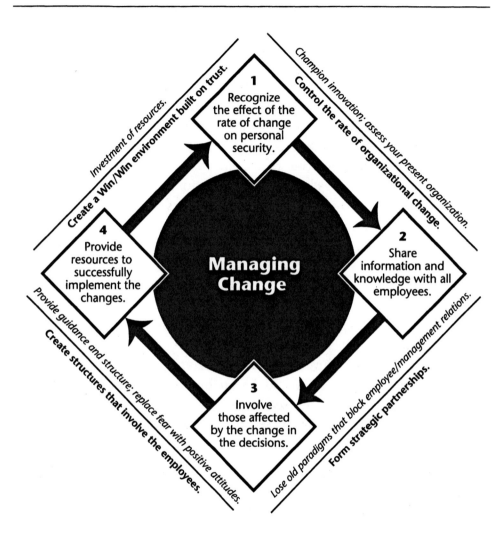

then introduced new technologies and new work methods into manufacturing and support areas. In 1989, the Palm Bay management team looked at the results of the innovations. Although there had been some success, human and physical resources had not been linked effectively. The goal was to achieve customer satisfaction through the synergistic interaction of all resources.

An opinion survey conducted at that time suggested that employees were ready for faster change. They wanted more satisfaction from their work, and they were willing to take on more responsibility. They wanted to take pride in achieving higher levels of customer satisfaction. To do this, employees would need to take ownership of their daily work and accept responsibility for continuous improvement. The management team agreed that the company needed to develop an organizational culture that would support those aspirations.

Harris's benchmarking studies suggested that a flexible, autonomous workplace would be more responsive to market needs. Rapid decision making on the production floor would translate into higher levels of quality and service. The people closest to the job would use their judgment and experience at the point of action. That strategy, although simple in concept, required major changes in the relationships among employees and their work, their co-workers, and their leaders.

Harris created several cross-functional teams that used a sociotechnological organizational design process focused on those issues. The Palm Bay plant's operations staff developed principles for the teams to use in redesigning the organization. The teams, which included employees from various levels and functions, had as a goal the design of a flexible, responsive organization that would become their customers' first choice in semiconductors. The new cultural environment would encourage employee participation, eliminate waste, reassign resources, and increase efficiencies. The outgrowth would be an organization offering world-class quality, cost, delivery, and service.

The team analyzed and redesigned the entire organization, including material and information flow, employee selection, and performance measurement and reward systems. After assessing the implications of their proposed design for their co-workers, they recommended a design and an implementation plan. After the management steering council accepted those recommendations, the company adopted them. The affected work groups' ability to master new skills set the pace for the changes. The change process required as much as five years for organization-wide adoption.

Healthy apprehension tempered employee enthusiasm for more control over day-to-day events. "What will my new role involve?" "What new skills will I need to learn?" "What training and other support is available?" "How will mistakes be handled?" The design and implementation processes anticipated those and many other questions. Frequent and open communications meetings assessed which approaches worked and which ones needed adjustment.

Step 2: Share Information and Knowledge with All Employees

This step is crucial in breaking paradigms that block effective employee–management relationships and helps establish an open and honest communication environment that forms the foundation for effective teamwork.

We have found that breaking down organizational barriers is a major challenge. Tom Peters (1988) advised making organizations "porous." He emphasized the importance of sharing information in a porous, boundaryless organization. The goal is a trust-based partnership with employees, and information sharing promotes trust. Information and knowledge drive change, and this step helps create an environment that anticipates questions related to organizational change. It also enhances the two-way communication necessary to reap the benefits of the self-directed work team concept.

Develop and Share a Vision

Stephen Covey (1991) wrote of the importance of a common vision in a principle-centered organization. When everyone has the same compass, no one needs to rely on a map (that is, on mechanistic procedures). We cannot overemphasize the importance of a common vision in a self-directed environment.

The first step in developing such a vision at Harris was to form a steering team of senior managers. Organizations with employee groups represented by collective bargaining agreements would add union leaders to such a steering team. The steering team's mission was to define and communicate the organization's shared purpose, vision for excellence, strategy, goals, and progress. It defined decision boundaries and broke down interdepartmental barriers. When a team understands the organization's business purpose, team members can focus on the important issues, but it is surprisingly easy to take employee awareness for granted. Our employee feedback showed that, although commitment and loyalty are vital, they are not enough. We must make sure there is no confusion about our business plans or about employees' roles in achieving them.

With that in mind, the steering team clearly defined the organization's vision. Employees had questions about their roles: "How do we want our stakeholders to view us in two, three, or five years?" "How will that image differ from today's?" "How would we operate if we were already achieving our vision?" "What are our core values as an organization, and do they need to change as we go forward?" "How would we behave if we were living those values truly?" "What do employees need to do?" "How will employees benefit from the change?"

Train Employees for Empowerment

The design phase of creating SDWTs required addressing many role, responsibility, and compensation issues. The organizational transformation required the SDWTs to accept responsibility and accountability for day-to-day production. Because sharing of knowledge must focus on developing employees in the proposed new work environment, and our employees needed to be competent in math and science, among other things, Harris provided such training when necessary.

Groups of employees volunteered for an intensive 12-month education program at a local community college. The classes took place at the work-site and on company time. This Specialized Employee Education (S.E.E.) program earned credit hours toward the college's associate's degree program. Employees who graduated from the S.E.E. program began to learn some equipment maintenance and process engineering skills. The goal was to empower production workers to take ownership of most aspects of their work.[2]

Sharing of information required many cultural changes. Information that was once reserved for management was now being made available to all employees. The Harris steering team diligently informed employees about target markets, products and services, competitive and organizational strategies, goals, measures, and progress. Monthly all-employee group meetings provided updates on those issues as well as on year-to-date financial results. The meetings also recognized successful teams and individuals. The process ensured that everyone knew Harris's business plans and how each employee was helping to achieve them. Everyone knew how the business was doing and what opportunities lay ahead.

As SDWTs mature, they need to learn and deploy increasingly sophisticated skills—a need that demands continual upgrading of an employee's skills. Sharing information and knowledge throughout the organization helps to develop a learning organization.

Promote an Understanding of Business Strategy and Finance

A learning organization must encourage employees to think like business owners. Training in business strategy and finance helps employees understand the overall business picture. Such knowledge prepared Harris's people to make better day-to-day business decisions on the factory floor. Harris used a board game called Zodiak[3] to give players the opportunity to manage the business and finances of a publicly held company by simulating business situations, placing employees in the chief executive officer's position, and letting them experience the results of their executive decisions.

In the game, players worked as a team to manage the fictitious, financially troubled Zodiak Industries through three business years. The teams made choices that affected cash flow, capital outlays, and earnings. Players guided Zodiak Industries from situation to situation and from fiscal quarter to fiscal quarter.

A follow-up survey to assess how Zodiak training affected employees' day-to-day decision making showed that

- 78 percent of respondents thought the training increased their understanding of business issues affecting the company.
- 68 percent felt the training helped them to see their job from a big-picture perspective.
- 71 percent said that internal business communications made more sense.
- 67 percent reported that the training helped their personal understanding of strategies and financial decisions.

Step 3: Involve Those Affected by Change in Designing the Change Process

People are more comfortable with change when they participate in planning for or implementing it. Participation in the change gives them a sense of control and reduces their fears. Change should be something that people *do*, not something that is done to them.

At Harris, much of the design work focused on changes at the production team level, including the transfer of some traditionally managerial responsibility to the new SDWTs. Although supervisors and first-level managers were aware of the organization design goals, the design content did not involve most of them personally.

This step enables the managers whom the change affects to guide and structure the change process. This empowering action delivers natural benefits and replaces fear of the unknown with a positive attitude toward change. As mentioned earlier, one of the few factors that management can influence during change is how fast it is carried out. This step also lays a solid base for enhancing trust and developing an environment more conducive to future changes.

A partnership between human resources development and the plant operations staff drove the implementation process. As the organization design phase ended, the plant operation and training managers took the lead. HRD provided consulting support.

To facilitate a transfer of ownership of the organizational changes, the following transition process was developed:

1. A plant steering committee, comprising HRD and plant personnel, was formed to support and guide the change process. Guidelines were set for monitoring the implementation process.

2. Local training resources and support in the form of facilities and training curriculum were provided. Facilitators acted as knowledge brokers to teams and management.

3. An off-site workshop exposed middle management to the SDWT concept and design to achieve management buy-in. The goal was to gain understanding and acceptance so that everyone was "singing from the same hymnal."

4. Implementation teams were formed at the departmental level to coach department employees through the change process.

5. Middle management received training on developing and enhancing interpersonal skills. They learned the importance of these skills for effective leadership of the change process.

6. A structured approach was implemented and followed with each team (the details of that approach will follow in chapter 8).

Step 4: Provide Resources to Implement the Change Successfully

Sufficient investment in resources is required to carry the change through successful implementation. Providing such resources also enhances trust and reduces the stress imposed by a limited resource environment.

Harris's steering team made a significant investment in people development. A new training department team focused primarily on the cultural change to teams. The training team provided support and facilitated all SDWT meetings. They also acted as knowledge brokers for both the work groups and management teams. Each SDWT that was created received resources to help it work through the following six-step development process:

1. *Purpose:* Why do we exist as a team?
2. *Vision:* What do we want to look like in the future?
3. *Goals and objectives:* What does the team need to accomplish?
4. *Strategy and tactics:* How does the team accomplish its goals and objectives?
5. *Roles and responsibilities:* What tasks are necessary, and who will do them? What responsibilities need to be transferred to the team, and when will that happen?
6. *Standards, norms, and expectations:* What rules guide our behaviors? How will the teams handle conflicts?

Various team-building exercises were developed to emphasize the role of relationship behaviors in team performance. We wrote a book documenting and providing activities for a team-building process: *50 Ways to Teach your Learner* (Rose and Buckley, 1999). The activities included are used at Harris sites around the world.

In 1995—about five years after the introduction of the team-based management system—Harris Semiconductor surveyed its 1,200 employees at the Palm Bay manufacturing site. Survey results showed that the four-step approach to organizational change was successful at Harris:

- 87 percent of the workforce favored the new SDWT structure.
- 96 percent of the workforce felt a need to contribute to the organizational goals, and they felt SDWTs provided the best structure for meeting that need.

- 100 percent of the employees felt that membership on a SDWT improved their self-esteem.
- 100 percent considered training important to the success of SDWTs.
- 95 percent stated that knowledge of where they were going as an organization and clear expectations were important to implementing SDWTs.
- 75 percent reported an improvement in attitude after implementing SDWTs.

The survey reflected a very positive attitude among employees, and the key ingredient to Harris's successful SDWT implementation was the effective management of change.

Organizational Change: Lessons Learned

Harris's experience shows how SDWTs can be implemented successfully with a structured approach. In their highly competitive global marketplace, teams provide vital flexibility, adaptive capability, and the speed to produce quality, cost, delivery, and service.

The success of Harris's change initiative can be linked to three key lessons. First, those closest to the work know best how to perform and improve their job. Second, most employees want to own their jobs and to understand how their jobs affect the organization's effectiveness. Third, teams provide opportunities for empowerment that would not be available in a traditional, hierarchical organization.

Companies must recognize that large-scale organizational changes (like converting to SDWTs) take time, energy, and commitment. Covey's Law of the Farm applies to change management. We cannot buy "instant teams" or "instant quality" ready-made. The farm teaches that we must plow, sow, and tend the crops before we can harvest. We have to nurture and support the implementation process before we can expect results.

Self-directed work teams can provide a definite competitive edge for businesses, allowing, if nothing else, speed in decision making. But we must empower workers with training and tools before we hand them responsibility. Training promotes morale and confidence at all levels of the organization, but an inadequate skill set can demoralize employees.

This chapter has presented Harris Semiconductor's experience in moving from a traditional management structure to a team-based management structure using a change model. It must be made perfectly clear that such a transition does not occur without a large investment in resources. The resources include training time and a dedicated training professional who will lead the process. The basic techniques for organizational change shared here will provide your organization with a model to help you on your journey to a team-based culture.

In Section II, we will focus on the type of training Harris used to accomplish the successful transition to a team-based culture.

Endnotes

1. The use of outside consultants who rely on canned, "one-size-fits-all" approaches, therefore, may be extremely perilous.

2. The idea behind IBM's workstation ownership program is similar.

3. Zodiak: The Game of Business Finance and Strategy is available from Paradigm Communications, 2701 North Rocky Point Drive, Suite 400, Tampa, FL 33607; 813.287.9330.

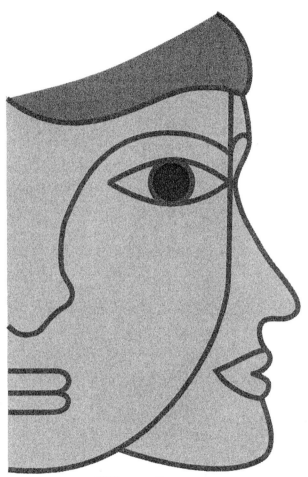

The Importance of Training:
Using the Trust-Leadership-
Competency Model

> Only now do I understand what my grandfather meant when he told me, "Son, the more you learn, you'll find the less you know."
>
> — Ed Rose

Chapter 5

Developing the Training

Ed Rose

The change to SDWTs requires resources and management support. Training must be focused on changing the organizational structure, the organizational culture, and employee behaviors.

First Steps

Many companies do not have specific training facilities on-site, so you will need to create a training organization or other resources that will focus on the transition. You also should identify a training facility within your organization. That facility will provide a place for teams to meet and receive their training. Creating such a training center is one of those "commitments to resources" mentioned in earlier chapters.

Next, appoint either full- or part-time facilitators who will use their understanding of the process to act as knowledge brokers. They will work with management and with the teams to ease the transition. The facilitator concentrates on the process so that the supervisor (team coordinator) can focus on his or her current role. That enables the supervisor to adopt the role of facilitator and coach, while the team accepts many of his or her administrative duties. The facilitator works closely with the direct supervisor or manufacturing leader to make this change go smoothly. The process usually takes some time and requires patience. The supervisor or leader must understand that his or her role is *changing*, not disappearing. Of course, the new organizational structure should need fewer coaches (team coordinators) than supervisors. Each organization should look for ways to use the supervisor's talents. Some companies have had great success using supervisors as trainers or in other functions.

When those preliminary issues are resolved, you should be ready to begin training within your organization. In this chapter, we will share with you the approach we took and the courses we developed to support the changing culture at Harris Semiconductor.

Teaching, Learning, and Involvement

The following outline is a good guide for team development, no matter what teaming structure you use. Harris Semiconductor called these sessions TLI: Teaching, Learning, Involvement. The information we present here should be sufficient for developing a training and education curriculum for your SDWT effort. Again, this book does not prescribe a one-size-fits-all solution. You will have to adapt Harris's experience to your situation. Use the classes listed as a guide for the training you want to provide within your organization. Some readers may find the number of classes we offered too few; others may consider the number too many. What your organization requires will depend entirely on your unique business environment.

TLI Session Structure

The TLI sessions' primary goal is to create self-directed work teams that improve quality continuously through structured problem solving and effective interpersonal communications. The training follows four phases of team development, as shown in Table 5.1. The classes in each phase guide the team through that development phase, but they are only a foundation and can be changed as appropriate. Those training classes focus on developing social, technical, and administrative skills:

- social classes focus on team members' interpersonal skills.
- technical classes provide the technical skills for self-sufficiency as a team.

Table 5.1
TLI Curriculum for Team Development

Skill Area	Phase I Classes	Phase II Classes	Phase III Classes	Phase IV Classes
Social	1. Team Dynamics (core), 8.0 hours (available in two-hour sessions) • Win–Win • Mutual Respect • Be Proactive • Listen • Synergy 2. Management of Change, 1.0 hour 3. Keirsey-Bates/Myers-Briggs Type Indicator, 1.5 hours 4. Conflict 101/Managing Conflict, 1.5 hours 5. What is TQM? 1.0 hour 6. Building Effective SDWTs, 4.0 hours	1. Effective Communication—"You Know What I Mean" Workshop, 1.5 hours 2. Conflict 102, 4.0 hours 3. Giving Constructive Feedback, 2.0 hours 4. Personal Action Plan for Teams, 1.5 hours 5. Listening 102, 4.0 hours 6. What Would You Do? (Part I), 3.0 hours 7. Stress Management, 4.0 hours 8. Team Profile, "Relationship Awareness Theory," 2.0 hours	1. What Would You Do? (Part II), 2.0 hours. 2. Paradigm Pioneers, 2.0 hours 3. Understanding and Managing Emotions, 1.5 hours 4. Opening the Door to Creativity, 4.0 hours 5. Effective Presentations, 4.0 hours 6. Sexual Harassment, 1.0 hour	1. Assertiveness Training. 2.0 hours 2. Creativity, the Look Beyond, 4.0 hours 3. "Attitude—Your Most Priceless Possession," 2.0 hours 4. Groupthink, 2.0 hours

(continued on next page)

Table 5.1
TLI Curriculum for Team Development *(continued)*

Skill Area	Phase I Classes	Phase II Classes	Phase III Classes	Phase IV Classes
Technical	1. Road map to Problem Solving (overview) (eight steps), 8.0 hours 2. Goal Alignment, 1.0 hour 3. Meeting Dynamics, 4.0 hours 4. SPC Training, 2.0 hours	1. Computer Training, 2.0 hours 2. Workstream (production logistics system) (as required), 2.0 hours 3. Key Plant Metrics, 1.0 hour 4. Level I Maintenance (as required) 5. TPM Training, 8.0 hours 6. Theory of Constraints, 4.0 hours	1. Train-the-Trainer, 4.0 hours 2. Waste Elimination Project, 2.0 hours 3. Level II Maintenance (as required)	1. Level III Maintenance, TBD 2. Business Simulation (core)—Zodiak, TBD 3. Failure Mode and Effects Analysis (FMEA), TBD
Administrative			1. Understanding Harris Policies and Procedures, 1.5 hours 2. Understanding Benchmarking (review only), 1.0 hour 3. Conducting Effective and Legal Interviews, 1.5 hours	1. Writing Team Members' Performance Reviews, 1.5 hours 2. Planning Budgets, Capital, and Labor, 1.5 hours

Note: SPC = statistical process control; TBD = to be determined; TLI = teaching, learning, involvement; TPM = total productive maintenance; TQM = total quality management.

- administrative classes focus on planning, scheduling, and general administrative duties of SDWTs.

Delivery of Classes

We recommend that classes be delivered to entire teams in segments of one-and-one-half to two hours. That allows scheduling flexibility and provides a vehicle for real-time team building. Class times should be set by the teams or by management in order to meet work schedules. Always strive to meet the customer's (that is, the team's) needs. The goal should be to provide whatever training resource a team requires. Each phase can take between 12 and 18 months to complete.

SDWTs require a tremendous commitment to training, including class development time, internal and external resources, and the time required for employees to attend classes. Make that necessary commitment clear to company executives who want to transition to SDWTs. After learning of the training investment required, some executives may decide not to make the transition.

This chapter documents the approach Harris Semiconductor has followed since 1989.

Course Descriptions

The following are course descriptions for classes developed to train Harris Semiconductor's SDWTs.

Phase I Social Courses

Team Dynamics

This class is the foundation of the interpersonal skills training for team development.

- *Purposes:* To teach the role of habits in teamwork; to improve team members by developing effective interpersonal habits.
- *Trainee's Objectives:* To understand effective interpersonal behaviors that support win-win interactions; to understand that effective teamwork requires a balance among relationship behaviors and task behaviors; to understand the need for an empathic listening style and to improve team member's listening skills; to recognize and

understand the power of paradigms; to understand the importance of developing trust within a team.

Note: The Leadership Game (see Tools for Trainers, page 170) can be used to facilitate discussion of unions and group dynamics.

Management of Change

Louis Martin-Vega developed this class to help employees understand the role of change in an organization.

- *Purpose:* To teach the importance of change, the rate of change, and its effect on companies and their employees.
- *Trainee's Objectives:* To understand the behavioral, psychological, and social factors of change; to increase team member's ability to be comfortable with change and understand how it affects people.

Keirsey-Bates or Myers-Briggs Type Indicator

This class helps each team member understand why people behave differently. Harris's Palm Bay plant primarily used the Keirsey-Bates course because it requires no certification for its instructors. Its validity is slightly lower than the MBTI assessment, but it has fewer questions and it requires less time to administer.

- *Purpose:* To give team members an understanding of the different human personality types and the strengths of each. The emphasis is on appreciating the differences in people, not on pigeonholing them.
- *Trainee's Objectives:* To use the strengths of the different personality types effectively within a team environment; to learn how to communicate effectively with the different types.

Conflict 101/Managing Conflict

This class helps team members understand that conflict is often unavoidable. Whether conflict is helpful or detrimental depends on how the team handles it. The class explores how conflict and disagreement can be helpful.

- *Purpose:* To teach how to recognize and manage conflict in a positive way.

- *Trainee's Objective:* To increase awareness of five ways to manage conflict. Team members learn that conflict is acceptable if it is managed properly and that constructive conflict, or mutually respectful disagreement, can produce positive results.

What Is TQM (Total Quality Management)?

This class provides a basic understanding of how we use TQM.

- *Purposes:* To teach TQM; to reinforce the basic company principles and values.
- *Trainee's Objective:* To develop a core understanding of the role of TQM in the Harris Semiconductor culture.

Building Effective SDWTs

This class is for all employees from senior management to production workers. It provides a basic understanding of the benefits of SDWT.

- *Purpose:* To enable participants to experience the difference between a traditional work environment and a team-based environment. In the simulation exercise, the team uses the six-step process detailed in chapter 8.
- *Trainee's Objective:* To learn the basic concepts behind the six-step approach. The simulation helps participants experience the benefits of SDWTs.

Note: The SDWT Game (see Tools for Trainers, page 166) can be modified to illustrate this point.

Phase I Technical Courses

Road Map to Problem Solving

This is a core class and a requirement for every team. It provides a basic problem-solving structure that all teams follow.

- *Purpose:* Provide a common problem-solving tool for teams.
- *Training Objective:* The Road Map to Problem Solving is a systematic approach that focuses on improving individual and team effectiveness. The class provides tools and techniques for identifying

and analyzing problems, including tools for brainstorming, analysis, and priority setting.

Note: Most companies use some particular problem-solving technique. The key question: Is that technique followed throughout the organization?

Goal Alignment

This class helps teams understand the importance of aligning sector goals with operational level team goals.

- *Purpose:* To identify what goal alignment is and how it works.
- *Trainee's Objectives:* To understand the importance of aligning team goals to department and division or sector goals; to understand the difference between goals and objectives.

Meeting Dynamics

This class was created to improve team meeting effectiveness. We have learned from experience that all employees in the organization need to attend this class, especially managers.

- *Purpose:* To provide team members with tools and techniques for holding effective meetings.
- *Trainee's Objectives:* To understand the components of meetings, agendas, and time constraints; to learn how to handle interaction problems constructively.

Note: Avoid using the statement "Meetings are where minutes are taken and hours are lost!"

SPC Training

This class is an overview of statistical process control for manufacturing processes. At Harris, SPC has been a major factor in standardization and maintenance of process quality.

- *Purpose:* To teach the importance of controlling the process.
- *Trainee's Objective:* To learn how SPC can be a valuable tool for controlling processes to ensure a quality product. Its application in the factory is taught, as is how to handle out-of-control points.

Phase II Social Courses

Effective Communication—"You Know What I Mean" Workshop

Richard Nixon said, "I know you believe you understand what you think I said; but I am not sure you realize that what you heard is not what I meant." Taking that as its motto, this class addresses the following elements of communication:

- Communication begins with what a person thinks he or she is saying, that is, the idea to be conveyed.
- Next we have what is actually said, not only through the words used but also through verbal emphasis and body language.
- Finally, we have what the listener thinks he or she heard the speaker say.

With so much going on in every exchange, we cannot overemphasize the importance of clear communication. This class helps team members appreciate the differences among various forms of communications. A videotape titled "You Know What I Mean" is the foundation for this session.[1]

- *Purpose:* To stress the importance of using two forms of communication in all circumstances.
- *Trainee's Objectives:* To understand the importance of clear communication; to understand the critical need for feedback in a communication process because feedback shows how the listener interpreted the message; to learn new skills for sending and receiving messages.

Conflict 102

This class was created because the teams wanted to know more about conflict. Our experience is that this is the most important subject for the teams to learn.

- *Purposes:* To continue the training in conflict resolution and to reinforce the five ways of managing disharmony learned in Conflict 101.
- *Trainee's Objective:* To experience a setting in which team members may resolve conflict in a nonthreatening environment.

Note: The Can We All Just Agree? exercise (see Tools for Trainers, page 175) can be modified to address conflict.

Giving Constructive Feedback

This class provides teams with a model for giving and receiving effective feedback.

- *Purpose:* To help team members distinguish between destructive and constructive feedback.
- *Trainee's Objective:* To develop effective skills for improving feedback techniques.

Personal Action Plan for Teams

This class shows how individuals with the proper attitude can make a difference in team success.

- *Purpose:* To teach how a positive attitude can be an asset on a team.
- *Trainee's Objectives:* To understand that each team member has a different role; to understand the importance of effective behaviors for team success.

Listening 101

- *Purpose:* To expand team members' listening skills.
- *Trainee's Objectives:* To develop a better understanding of the art of listening to others; to improve listening skills.

What Would You Do? (Part I)

This class tests the knowledge level of the work team.

- *Purposes:* To provide insight into the various daily issues facing SDWTs; to provide real-life situations and let the team decide what to do.
- *Trainee's Objectives:* To experience firsthand how teams make decisions on a day-to-day basis; to experience the impact of decisions.

Stress Management

This class helps team members deal with stress in their daily lives, and was developed by Harris employee assistance program professionals who specialize in this type of subject matter.

- *Purpose:* To teach how to deal with stress in a team environment as well as outside of work.
- *Trainee's Objective:* To learn techniques to reduce stress inside and outside the work environment.

Team Profile

This course uses the Relationship Awareness Theory[2] to teach a different way of looking at team behaviors.

- *Purpose:* To provide an easy method for team members to understand the various behaviors displayed by other team members.
- *Trainee's Objective:* To create a tool that is easy to use.

Note: The MBTI instrument also can be used to profile a team. Other useful tools include the Style of Teamwork Inventory and the Teamwork Appraisal Survey.[3]

Phase II Technical Courses

Computer Training

This is a set of training classes to increase computer skills for team members and to update and add classes as needed to stay current in technology. Harris used an outside training organization to provide these courses.

- *Purpose:* To provide team members with skills to improve individual and team performance.
- *Trainee's Objective:* To learn various software programs to improve team competencies.

Workstream

This class reviews the in-house production control and logistics system, Workstream.

- *Purpose and Objective:* To help team members fully understand and use the in-house production management system.

Key Plant Metrics

This class reviews the key plant metrics with teams. Because performance measurements drive behavior in every organization, people must understand those measurements and relate them to their activities.

- *Purpose:* To teach team members what the key plant metrics are and why they exist.
- *Trainee's Objective:* To learn clear measurements for SDWT performance so the team can check its own performance.

Level 1 Maintenance

This class develops maintenance skills in the factory.

- *Purpose:* To train team members on minor maintenance skills that management identifies for transfer to the teams.
- *Trainee's Objective:* To learn skills to elevate each team's skill competencies.

TPM (Total Productive Maintenance) Training

This class provides a basic understanding of the TPM concept and its tools (Figure 5.1). Because the operators who do the job every day are often in the best position to detect and correct abnormalities, the goal is to have them perform routine maintenance tasks like cleaning and inspection.

- *Purposes:* To train all employees in the concepts and tools of TPM; to equip them to improve effectiveness.
- *Trainee's Objective:* To increase knowledge of the techniques of TPM.

Theory of Constraints (TOC)

This class provides a general overview of the TOC.

- *Purposes:* To teach the concepts and techniques of TOC; to focus all employees on improving the constraints.
- *Trainee's Objectives:* To develop an understanding of how TOC and TPM work together.

Note: There are several simulation games on the market that illustrate this concept very well. "The Goal" videotape[4] from the Goldratt Institute is also a useful tool.

Phase III Social Courses

What Would You Do? (Part II)

This class is a follow-up to Part I. Real-life team issues require responses by team members. A scoring system provides a baseline for team feedback.

Figure 5.1
TPM Road Map

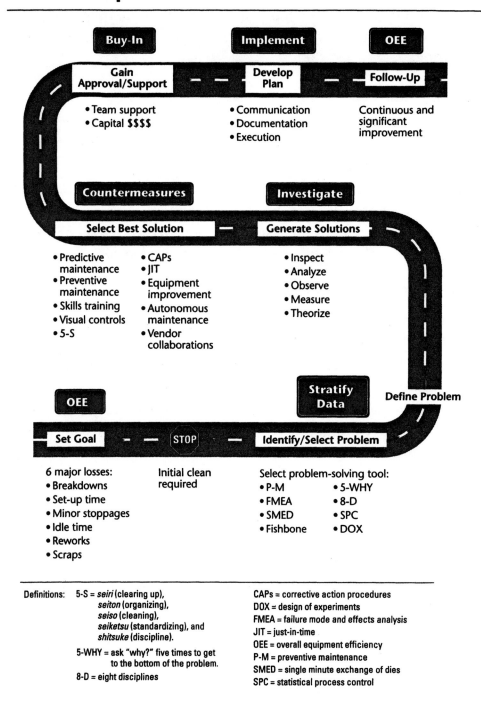

Buy-In		Implement		OEE

Gain Approval/Support — **Develop Plan** — **Follow-Up**

- Team support
- Capital $$$$

- Communication
- Documentation
- Execution

Continuous and significant improvement

Countermeasures		Investigate

Select Best Solution — **Generate Solutions**

- Predictive maintenance
- Preventive maintenance
- Skills training
- Visual controls
- 5-S

- CAPs
- JIT
- Equipment improvement
- Autonomous maintenance
- Vendor collaborations

- Inspect
- Analyze
- Observe
- Measure
- Theorize

OEE		**Stratify Data**	Define Problem

Set Goal — — (STOP) — — **Identify/Select Problem**

6 major losses:
- Breakdowns
- Set-up time
- Minor stoppages
- Idle time
- Reworks
- Scraps

Initial clean required

Select problem-solving tool:
- P-M
- FMEA
- SMED
- Fishbone
- 5-WHY
- 8-D
- SPC
- DOX

Definitions: 5-S = *seiri* (clearing up), *seiton* (organizing), *seiso* (cleaning), *seiketsu* (standardizing), and *shitsuke* (discipline).

5-WHY = ask "why?" five times to get to the bottom of the problem.

8-D = eight disciplines

CAPs = corrective action procedures
DOX = design of experiments
FMEA = failure mode and effects analysis
JIT = just-in-time
OEE = overall equipment efficiency
P-M = preventive maintenance
SMED = single minute exchange of dies
SPC = statistical process control

Source: Randy Dunbar, Andre Blanc, and Steve Buckley, Harris Semiconductor.

- *Purpose:* To provide an excellent experiential tool with which all team members may practice interaction.
- *Trainee's Objectives:* To understand the impact of making effective team decisions; to have additional experience with actual decision making.

Paradigm Pioneers

This class helps team members understand risk taking in an organization and the role they may choose to play. It uses Joel Barker's videotape, "Paradigm Pioneers."[5]

- *Purpose:* To focus on how paradigms affect team and organizational performance.
- *Trainee's Objective:* To understand the organizational roles of the "settler" and the "pioneer," as defined in the videotape.

Understanding and Managing Emotions

This class helps team members understand and control their emotions in a team environment.

- *Purpose:* To teach team members how to recognize and manage their emotions in team activities.
- *Trainee's Objectives:* To understand that emotions are manageable; to use effective techniques to manage anger; to recognize potential problems in team activities.

Opening the Door to Creativity

This class offers "a journey into possibility." Growth and development require change, change requires risk and lateral thinking techniques, and those produce creativity.

- *Purpose:* To promote a discussion of creativity and the development of an environment that allows it to flourish.
- *Trainee's Objectives:* To understand creative thinking; to recognize his or her own creative abilities; to experience breaking out of self-limiting behavior and looking for possibilities, challenges, and opportunities; to increase capacity to generate new ideas.

Effective Presentations

- *Purpose:* To examine the elements of an effective presentation and their application (basic skills).
- *Trainee's Objectives:* To analyze the speaking situation; to plan effectively for both team and personal presentations; to use the provided tools and techniques in presentations; to overcome nervousness.

Sexual Harassment

- *Purpose:* To teach team members the proper conduct in working relationships among co-workers; to review sexual harassment laws.
- *Trainee's Objective:* To recognize exactly what constitutes sexual harassment.

Phase III Technical Courses

Train-the-Trainer

- *Purpose:* To cover specific training elements, including the adult learning process, needs and performance, and materials development.
- *Trainee's Objectives:* To learn to train others in the art of training; to understand how adults learn; to use course techniques to improve training skills.

Waste Elimination Project

In this class, team members actively participate in a waste elimination project in their geographic area.

- *Purpose:* To identify the most prominent causes of waste in local auto manufacturing facilities.
- *Trainee's Objectives:* To learn about Imai's seven deadly wastes;[6] to understand the value of reducing waste in all situations.

Level II Maintenance

- *Purpose:* To provide additional training to improve team members' maintenance skills.

- *Trainee's Objective:* To learn to perform maintenance tasks to the levels of criteria defined by the department steering committee.

Phase III Administrative Courses

Understanding Harris Policies and Procedures

- *Purpose:* To review Harris policies and procedures for identified issues.
- *Trainee's Objective:* To learn Harris policies and procedures.

Understanding Benchmarking

- *Purpose:* To review why benchmarking is important and how a company benchmarks other companies.
- *Trainee's Objectives:* To identify the seven-step process of benchmarking; to evaluate the benefits of breakthrough thinking; to participate in benchmarking activities.

Conducting Effective and Legal Interviews

- *Purpose:* To teach employees how to avoid legal problems during the hiring process.
- *Trainee's Objective:* To learn to conduct legal interviews.

Note: Harris involves frontline workers in the interview process because new employees must fit into the team environment. SDWT workers can often provide a perspective that supervisors and HRD personnel do not have. It is easy to ask illegal questions about marital status, religion, and so on without having ill intentions, but interviewers must avoid doing that.

Phase IV Social Courses

Assertiveness Training

- *Purpose:* To teach the role of positive assertiveness in helping individuals become strong team players.
- *Trainee's Objectives:* To understand the difference between assertive, passive, and aggressive behaviors (assertive behavior is usually constructive; passive and aggressive behaviors are not); to

know how to assert ideas constructively to convert them to actions because even the best ideas are not useful unless their developers convince others to act on them; to understand that differences of opinion often expose problems or opportunities that would have otherwise remained hidden.

Creativity, The Look Beyond

- *Purpose:* To introduce "out-of-the-box thinking" and lateral thinking, which teach us how to view things as a whole and how to dig even deeper to discover our hidden levels of creativity.
- *Trainee's Objectives:* To attack problems using team learning, which improves the group dynamics of dialog and discussion; to use lateral thinking to create without judging. (Linear thinking, which is characteristic of mathematics and similar disciplines, requires each process step to be correct. But the need to assess each step can stifle creativity. Lateral thinking requires only that the final answer be correct.)

Attitude: Your Most Priceless Possession

Attitudes are habits; we are not born with them, and we can change them.

- *Purpose:* To teach the importance of team members' attitudes in developing strong relationships.
- *Trainee's Objectives:* To assess the effects of individual attitudes toward other team members; to understand how each person's attitude affects a team's success or failure.

Groupthink

Groupthink is an organizational dysfunction, the symptoms of which are complete harmony and agreement. Everybody is thinking alike, which means that nobody is thinking. It is organizational hubris.

- *Purpose:* To teach teams in Phase IV to avoid groupthink.
- *Trainee's Objectives:* To understand the value of different opinions in teamwork; to recognize the negative effects of groupthink on teams and organizations; to recognize the danger signs of

groupthink, including feelings of invincibility and the belief that competitors are evil or inferior.

Phase IV Technical Courses

Level III Maintenance

- *Purpose:* To continue team members' training in equipment maintenance.
- *Trainee's Objective:* To perform to criteria defined by the department steering committee.

Zodiak—The Game of Business Finance and Strategies

The course uses the imaginary Zodiak Industries to present a simple picture of how a business operates, and then relates that model to Harris Semiconductor's operations. It gives everyone at Harris Semiconductor a common, basic understanding of the financial and strategic business issues involved in running the company. Participants learn the "big picture" of business through discovery learning (rather than lecture) as they play the three-year simulation game.

- *Purpose:* To provide skill training in the following topics and associated behaviors: quality commitment, planning and organizing, business decision making, and teamwork.
- *Trainee's Objectives:* To understand financial terms and key indicators like cash flow, return on assets, return on equity, and profit margins; to understand the impact of strategic business decisions (just-in-time production management, quality management, continuous improvement, research and development, resource utilization, customer relations, and so on).

Failure Mode and Effects Analysis (FMEA)

FMEA is a systematic technique for listing failure modes, and rating their severity and causes, their chances of occurrence, and their chances of detection. Ratings follow a 1-to-10 scale, and the risk priority number (RPN) is their product. Prevention and improvement activities obviously should focus on modes with high RPNs. The Automotive Industry Action Group's publication *Potential Failure Mode and Effects Analysis*

(1995) provides additional technical detail, probably beyond the level required by operators. The Ford Motor Company is an excellent resource for this type of training.

- *Prerequisite:* TPM training
- *Purpose:* To help a team understand problems that can arise with process equipment.
- *Trainee's Objectives:* To identify a problem piece of equipment; to put systems in place to eliminate the problem(s); to write the first document to indicate the potential problem(s).

Phase IV Administrative Training

Writing Team Members' Performance Reviews

- *Prerequisites:* Effective Communication, Giving Constructive Feedback
- *Purpose:* To help team members develop the skills necessary to write team peer evaluations.
- *Trainee's Objectives:* To understand the difference between subjective and objective information; to recognize that descriptions must be specific and complete; to learn to focus on the issues and not on the person; to know how to write constructively.

Planning Budgets, Capital, and Labor

- *Purpose:* To teach team members how to prepare department budgets.
- *Trainee's Objective:* To learn to prepare department budgets.

In this chapter we've described the scope of training necessary for SDWTs. Use the information presented here as a point of reference and develop classes tailored to the demand of your business environment. At the Harris Semiconductor Palm Bay facility, each department has a steering committee that selects the required classes for the teams, but teams also may request extra classes. Facilitators and HRD professionals conduct all of the soft skill-type training. The facilitators are members of the newly established manufacturing training department; they serve as knowledge brokers for the teams and help them in their transition to SDWTs.

Additional training resources you may consider include *Creating Training Miracles* by Alastair Rylatt and Kevin Lohan (ASTD, 1998), and *Training Design and Delivery* by Geri E. McArdle (ASTD, 1999). I strongly recommend a visit to squarewheels@compuserve.com, a Website developed by Scott Simmerman. One tool available there, Square Wheels, is designed to generate action learning, reflective perspective, participatory involvement, and a sense of ownership. Some of the Square Wheels illustrations have specific themes and messages, but most of them can have various meanings and linkages. The general themes include managing and leading change, continuous quality improvement, coaching for improved performance, creativity, systems thinking, personal growth and development, productivity improvement, and leadership and facilitation skills.

Endnotes

1. Obtained originally from Rank Roundtable, but possibly no longer available.

2. Available from Personal Strengths Publishing Co., Box 397, Pacific Palisades, CA 90272.

3. Available from Teleometrics International, www.teleometrics.com; 800-527-0406.

4. Available from North River Press, Croton-on-Hudson, NY.

5. Available from Charthouse International Learning Corp., www.charthouse.com.

6. Imai (1997) describes seven forms of *muda,* or waste: overproduction, inventory, motion, rejects/repair, processing, waiting, and transportation.

A good motto is, "Always tell the truth;
it is always easier to remember."
— Ed Rose

Chapter 6

TLC: The Role of Trust, Leadership, and Competency

Ray Odom

We've seen that change is often difficult and sometimes traumatic for people and organizations. People resist change unless they see a compelling reason for it, and even then they frequently are reluctant to accept it. Some see change as threatening to their personal security. Others have vested interests in the existing system. Trust, leadership, and competency (TLC) play key roles in the change process and are significant factors in moving an organization toward self-directed work teams.

Management Commitment

Management commitment and leadership are overwhelmingly the most critical factors in any cultural change. Cultural change begins with the personal commitment and the active involvement of senior management. There are few or no examples of successful cultural change that did not have senior management's active involvement. Management leadership must go far beyond the typical rhetoric found in many companies. It must guide the organization not only by words, but by example. Management must define improvement plans and goals, then review and reward their successful achievement. That is a key point: *The performance measurement system you implement must reward desired behaviors.* Management must provide the resources and remove the obstacles that keep the organization and its employees from reaching their full potential.

Leadership in the Change Process

Leadership must set a framework and an atmosphere for organizational learning. It must then communicate, motivate, and move the organization toward improvements that promote success. Management decides what needs to happen, sets priorities, deals with larger systemic problems, listens to the customer, and drives the creation of new products and services. Employees must be empowered and trained so they can solve problems, control their work, and improve their jobs.

Case Study: Management Leadership at Harris Semiconductor

Harris Semiconductor assessed its TQM structure in 1991 and found that it had over 200 teams. There were many TQM "pockets of excellence," but the company generally seemed to be experiencing team gridlock. Management needed to assess what the teams were doing because the company had priorities that needed more focus and attention. Management discovered that most teams did not know the key priorities, and many of the problems getting attention were not linked to those key priorities. Some employees were members of several teams, all focused on different projects. To achieve better alignment, the senior management team formed a Quality Council, defined the top five business priorities, and communicated those priorities throughout the organization. The focus of every team and every individual contributor was reoriented to address one or several of those key priorities.

Communications

Today, Harris issues a formal communication package monthly to every department manager at every site. Each manager is responsible for reviewing and communicating the contents of the package to all employees, face-to-face. Those reviews usually take the form of a monthly communications meeting. The information presented includes company values, mission, vision, market strategy, and business priorities. For each priority, there are defined measures with goals, including "stretch" goals, for the year. Charts for each priority are updated monthly to show how the company is performing against its goals and are displayed prominently at all sites.

Senior managers, including the president, visit each plant semiannually. They meet with employees on all shifts and deliver the message personally. Occasionally, those meetings are turned into celebrations to recognize recent successes. It's important to celebrate success whenever you can.

Commitment to Goals

To promote strategic linkage and alignment, Harris Semiconductor established a goal deployment process. A primary objective was to make the process easy to use by all managers responsible for goal deployment. The Deming Plan–Do–Check–Act cycle was adopted as a basic model for continuous improvement. We simply positioned goal deployment as a bridge between the "Plan" and "Do" steps in the continuous improvement process. During each annual planning process, senior managers review and revise the business priorities and goals. Managers at the next level are then brought into the process to determine how best to achieve those priorities and goals. Similar level-to-level interaction continues down the organization until there are actionable goals set for every SDWT, every project improvement team, and every individual contributor. The process promotes alignment with the key priorities throughout every function in the organization.

At Harris Semiconductor, a senior manager serves as champion for each priority area. The champion's role is to work with management teams across the entire organization to deploy the assigned priority goal.

Steering councils are useful for change initiatives, serving to drive the alignment process. The councils also can sponsor improvement teams to solve specific problems or systemic issues. When a problem is solved, a team is recognized by the steering council and then it disbands. The steering council comprises management and cross-functional representatives, thereby offering the advantage of many organizational perspectives.

That is only one example of a process to promote organizational alignment. It is crucial that you choose a process and a structure that work for your organization.

Training and Development

In chapter 5, the authors discussed skills that a self-managed work team needs. Organizations must invest in training resources to ensure employee competency for success. Management must provide the resources to ensure that effective change takes place—and a part of those resources is required to create and maintain training at all levels.

Rewards and Recognition

At Harris, award and recognition programs are sponsored by management to reinforce desired behaviors. Employee teams often participate in developing those programs. As part of the recognition programs, employees can receive modest payouts—usually gift certificates—for their individual or team's contribution to achieving a business priority. Recognition can come from co-workers or management. Categories of recognition include customer satisfaction, quality improvement, teamwork, and innovation.

The company introduced a major reward system change in 1994. In addition to base pay and the employee benefits package, the company added a third component to its total compensation package—variable pay based on net income. The company issues a cash lump-sum payout to all eligible employees if the business achieves or beats its annual net income target. In 1994, everyone was eligible to receive a 4 percent end-of-year cash bonus. The bonus also could double to 8 percent if the business achieved 150 percent of its income target. The plan allowed for the payout target to increase from 4 percent to 10 percent over several years.

The variable pay program encourages teamwork and goal alignment across the sector. The compensation program shares the business's success with all of the employees involved in making the business successful.

Training and Financial Performance

Harris encourages employees to meet customers' expectations, increase sales, and reduce costs to improve net income. A business training class, Zodiak, was developed to improve employees' understanding of the financial aspects of the business. In that eight-hour workshop, employees learn the basics of finance, including such topics as income statements, balance sheets, cash flow, and financial ratios. Zodiak uses a board game approach to make it more interactive and to simplify the learning process. The training is intended to improve employees' financial knowledge so that correct decisions can be made at all levels in the organization to improve the bottom line. To make it even more interactive, two members of the management group facilitate each workshop.

Role of Trust in the Change Process

What do employees want from management during any change process? Above all, they want honesty. Integrity, ethical behavior, and trustworthiness are never to be compromised. Be open and candid. Do not make a promise you can't keep.

Leaders must think beyond the daily routine, convey their vision for a better future, and not dwell on the past. Employees look to leaders who are inspiring and motivational. They want to believe all parties have a common interest. Regular and direct interaction is important. Manage by walking around and showing personal enthusiasm.

Remember that people are often uncomfortable with change. They will feel more secure if they are confident in management's competence. The leaders must show commitment to continuous improvement and a willingness to teach *and* learn. Leaders must recognize that an organization is only as good as its people.

Successful Leadership

There are four levels of leadership and a guiding principle for each level (Covey, 1991). *Trust* and *trustworthiness* are the guiding principles for personal and interpersonal leadership, respectively. *Empowerment* is the key principle for management leadership. *Alignment* is the key principle for organizational leadership.

A manager must understand the needs of his or her people. People need to feel in control of their own work. They must understand how their work is valuable to the company—that every task has significance. People want challenging work and opportunities for lifelong learning.

They also want feedback, another intrinsic motivator, and recognition for their contributions. Organize so people can help themselves, their customers, and the bottom line. If you organize around your people's needs, you will usually meet your customers' needs. There must be more focus on pleasing customers than on pounding the competition. Focusing on quality, cost, delivery, and service will contribute greatly to business success. Once people are empowered, they feel ownership for achieving results, and when your people succeed, your business succeeds. That concept, when applied to the internal organization, is equally powerful—it is where the SDWT organizational structure plays a key role.

It is vital to align all improvement activities and business priorities to achieve business success. A simple (but structured) goal deployment process is the best way to get everyone aiming at and hitting the right targets consistently.

The best way to improve your leadership style is to know yourself. Know your strengths and capitalize on them. Do not let a strength become a weakness by overusing that strength. Know your deficiencies and your blind spots and strive to improve them. When dealing with others, be a good learner and a good teacher, and convey a consistent message. Be visible and approachable. Remember that people have different perspectives of you, so seek feedback from your boss, your peers, and your subordinates.

Change management requires personal leadership skills. If you don't know how to lead, you must learn. And while you're at it, train other managers around you. Don't settle for evolutionary improvements; demand revolutionary expectations. Your competition is not waiting for you to catch up. Train employees in the methods and tools of improvement, and get some training yourself. Recognize that there are some tasks that you cannot and must not delegate. Participate in the organizational change steering process and the deployment process. When something is done well, be there personally to recognize the people involved. Organizations must change their reward systems to drive the right behaviors, but don't wait until those systems are changed before starting the implementation.

As an HRD training professional, you are a leader in your organization. It is important not only for senior managers to embrace TLC, but also for you in your role as champion and facilitator to understand the long-term effects of TLC. As Andrew Carnegie said, "People pay more attention to what you do and less attention to what you say." Your actions (that is, your leadership) are absolutely necessary for the successful implementation of any major organizational change.

About the Author

Ray Odom is vice president and general manager of space and defense products for Harris Semiconductor. He is a graduate of the University of Florida, where he earned a bachelor of science degree in electrical engineering, and is also a graduate of the Harris-University of Florida Graduate Program in Business. Odom has authored numerous publications on subjects ranging from manufacturing methods to team-based organizations.

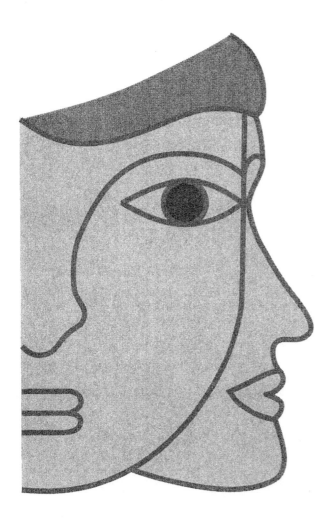

Implementing Self-Directed Work Teams

Now is the only moment with any power
in my life.

— Lewis Losoncy
Today! Grab It: Seven Vital Attitude
Nutrients to Build the New You

Chapter 7

Designing the Change Process

Steve Gilmore

In this chapter, my goal is to provide the thought processes to prepare you for the transition to self-directed work teams, using details of Harris Semiconductor's design process. Use this chapter to orient your thoughts to implementing the transition to team-based management. By this point in the book, you should know if your organization has a need for SDWTs and is ready to implement them.

In the preceding two sections, we have stressed the importance of committing resources and providing direction. Now, before addressing the specific details of an implementation, we must recognize that success depends on the basic principles of behavioral change. Here we will focus on how management should move in this change process. People and organizations naturally tend to fear and resist change, but in business change is necessary to remain competitive and viable. To overcome resistance and create a future that embraces collective organizational change, the change agents must make clear to employees why change is necessary and desirable.

The Need for Management Commitment

A successful transition to SDWTs requires time, money, and management commitment. Slogans and motivational speeches alone cannot produce results. In the absence of commitment, management will degrade the workforce's confidence in the change process. When managers or executives give only lip service to any new change being implemented, they are using some very ancient psychological techniques against their own organization.

The commentator Li Ch'uan told a story to illustrate this principle in *The Art of War* (1983), written by the Chinese general, Sun Tzu. When Duke Chuang of Lu was preparing for battle, he heard his enemies beat their drums. He wanted to attack them immediately, but his advisor Ts'ao Kuei counseled him to wait. The enemy drums rolled again, and later yet again. "Now attack them," Ts'ao Kuei urged, and the duke ordered an assault. After the duke had won, Ts'ao Kuei explained, "In battle, a courageous spirit is everything. Now the first roll of the drum tends to create this spirit, but with the second it is already on the wane, and after the third it is gone altogether. I attacked when their spirit was gone and ours was at its height."

In business, management often beats the drums to announce a new quality initiative. The workers are eager and excited at the beginning, but when nothing happens, they lose their enthusiasm and their morale drops. It's like getting an athletic team geared up for a game and then postponing it.

Don't beat the drums unless you mean it. That applies to any quality improvement initiative, not only to SDWTs.

Management does not have to increase head count or throw money at the organizational change to show its commitment. By the same token, a management team that is unwilling to commit the necessary resources should not try to implement self-directed teams. Harris reorganized and effectively redeployed its existing number of workers, and they achieved their desired results. The dedication of resources is an investment in the company's future.

Getting Started: Defining the Change

Once the organization has decided to change its basic culture, it must put the necessary structures in place. As we noted earlier, change is something that people should do, not something that is done to them. Effective change management involves the people whom the change affects, and communication is a key starting point.

Communication provides a common framework that enhances ownership of the process. Start by identifying the organization's function, then ask why it needs to change, what needs to change, and into what it should change. How should the changes happen? Will the change address a core strategic business process like marketing and sales, manufacturing, or research and development? Or, will the change focus on a more defined, tactical process such as order entry, accounts receivable, or employee records? The proper change strategy depends on several internally or externally driven variables.

Know the Environment, Your Competitors, and Yourself

Change is an adaptation to evolving competitive circumstances, including the competitive environment and the opponents. Sun Tzu (1963, 1983) advised his readers, "Know the enemy and know yourself." That is, understand the characteristics of your and your competitors' organizations. Benchmark and learn from what other people are doing, but do not imitate blindly. Adopt techniques and methods that will work well for *your* organization. In benchmarking terminology, look for the "enabler" that makes something work for other organizations

Sun Tzu also stressed the need to understand the competitive environment. Today that environment includes market barriers like economy of scale, distribution channels, customer switching costs, and the production learning curve. It also includes dynamic factors like business cycles and currency exchange rates. Knowing the environment and its competitors helps an organization understand why and how it should change.

Consider your competitive environment. Some organizations repeatedly introduce new products and services; others are slow to develop new offerings. What is the difference between them? Why do some enjoy steadily growing market share and others find their competitive positions eroding? Some markets are experiencing rapid or even explosive growth, and there is plenty of room for everybody. In mature markets, however, the pie isn't getting any bigger; the only way to get a bigger piece is to take someone else's share. Compare your company's performance to industry leaders in general and to those in your industry in particular. Do you enjoy a strategic competitive advantage? Are your customers delighted with your product portfolio? Do they like your value-added pricing, or your delivery and service?

A healthy organization not only considers the external environment, it also assesses and responds to changing demands on its internal capacity, competencies, skills, systems, structure, and culture. Are the management team and employees ready for change? Do people view the organizational systems as responsive to customer expectations? Who is responsible for the current business processes and procedures? Who should be responsible for ensuring rapid responses to potential customer issues? Is information available to the right people at the right time? Does organizational behavior reflect a shared value system, and is that value system consistent with the organization's vision? Answers to those questions are part of "knowing yourself."

Management Leadership and Organizational Vision

The management team usually comprises those who are accountable for the business process being changed. The team must have the power to make most of the change decisions and to provide financial and human resources. After assessing the internal and external environment and benchmarking competitors, the management team defines the desired state: "Where do we want to go?" In its leadership role, the team defines the future vision. How does it want the organization's stakeholders to view the company in two to three years, or three to five years? How does that vision differ from the current status? Do the organization's core values support the vision, and what kind of behavior will they drive?

As leaders, the team initially communicates the principles that will guide the change process. It reinforces the vision frequently. Often there must be an incubation period in which employees clarify the vision's meaning and implications. Effective leadership recognizes people's desire to align their activities freely with a cause they understand and to which they relate.

As workers buy into the vision, management must display commitment by planning the required operational and organizational systems. It is not enough simply to understand system requirements and address existing capability shortfalls. The logical integration of the technical and human systems is a critical step.

Involve Others

High-impact teams are designed around work processes that can deliver outstanding customer satisfaction. Teams need capable processes and feedback on results as well as process performance. Feedback is a key aspect of intrinsic motivation—the motivation that makes the job its own reward. A team must have the knowledge, skill, and authority to act on the feedback, and it must be accountable for results. It is the management team's role to involve in the planning process the people who will own the results of the design effort.

In organizations with collective bargaining agreements, the union must be an active participant in the change process. The union and the management team must share concerns openly and agree on the change process. Remember, change is not something that management should do to people or to their work structure. People are far more receptive to change when they participate in planning for it. In all cases, change agents must define decision boundaries and communicate them to the design team.

Design Teams

Employees and managers should participate jointly in creating the new organizational structure. Cross-level and cross-functional teams often produce the best organizational system for promoting quality, value, delivery, and service to internal and external customers.

In large-scale business process redesign, design team membership should include a diagonal slice of the affected organizations. The design team must incorporate disciplines like finance, sales, engineering, manufacturing, human resources, and customer service. Cross-functional teams are common in technical activities like design for manufacture. They are also vital in organizational system design. The team should include a variety of nonexempt, exempt professional, and management personnel. That helps maintain a broad, multiorganizational-level perspective. For intact natural work groups, those involved in the day-to-day team activities are free to consult with internal subject matter experts.

At the big-picture level, work teams must believe that their efforts truly affect customer satisfaction, so teams should receive responsibility for significant pieces of business processes.

Technical System Evaluation

Over time, any work process experiences variation in expected outcome. Identify and evaluate key variation sources in the current process. Analyze the root cause(s) of the variation and the current control systems. If root causes cannot be eliminated, then control systems must alert the team in a timely and meaningful way.

Evaluation of the existing system often is the most difficult phase because the change process questions methods that people long have accepted as the "right way" to do things. Identifying and selecting corrective actions to reduce variation may require testing, adjustment, and retesting to get it right. This is the plan–do–check–act improvement cycle. During that phase, the design team often uses process flowcharting, customer interviews, analysis of performance trends, statistical process management tools, and benchmarking. Several benchmarking trips may be necessary to gather data.

The design team reviews the results of the technical system design phase with the sponsoring management team. Their review focuses on clarifying the design's assumptions, supporting data, analysis, conclusions, and recommendations. Those recommendations that are likely to add value become the template for the human system design phase.

Human System Evaluation

An organization's human system refers to the organizational structure, team member skills, decision-making boundaries, and support systems. Setting aside the norms and values of the current culture presents a constant challenge during this phase. Questions to be answered in designing new human systems include the following:

- What is the best way to organize people around the work?
- How will roles and responsibilities change?
- What skills do people need to perform the new work?
- How many people will be on the team?
- Do they have the necessary skills, or will they need training?
- What information will the team need, and where will it come from?
- What are the team's decision boundaries?
- How will the team make decisions?
- How will the team set goals and measure improvement?
- How will success be recognized and rewarded?
- How will team members continue to develop as individuals as well as team members?

The answers to some of those questions will come from the management and some will come from the design team. Chapter 9 will guide you through the process of answering those questions in an orderly fashion.

Planning the Changes

The management team should encourage the design team to strive for breakthrough thinking. Sustainable change, however, may require an evolutionary implementation strategy to overcome unforeseen obstacles like hidden resistance. Plans for incremental change require sufficient detail to bring about observable progress. The management team plays an active role in defining and monitoring these plans.

Once the necessary changes are identified, the design team creates an implementation plan. That plan considers not only the procedural changes but also potential barriers to change. The team defines strategies to reduce or remove such barriers and identifies resource requirements such as additional capital for personal computers, budget for change-over, skills training, and people. The team also must establish a schedule that identifies the steps along the way to keep the process moving forward.

Key Issues in the Design Phase

Before structuring and starting an implementation process, it is useful to emphasize the following key issues for the design phase:

1. *Delegate the responsibility only when the team is ready.* Transfer of working responsibility to the team itself occurs as the team's skill level increases. The design phase must contemplate the need to identify when a team is ready to assume the responsibility. Implementation should include transfer milestones for both time and activity. The six steps to implementation of SDWTs discussed in chapter 8 will help in this process.

2. *Coaching a team to success does not mean abdicating all responsibility.* Just as for a parent raising a child from infancy through adolescence to adulthood, a trainer's coaching responsibility does not disappear; it merely diminishes gracefully with time.

3. *Pace the rate of change to the ability of the team.*

4. *Know the team configuration that you plan to develop.*

With those key points in mind, we can move on to the implementation process from the team's perspective. The next chapter will provide you with a step-by-step process for developing individual teams. It will allow you, as a training professional, to facilitate the development of any type of team in your organization.

About the Author

Steve Gilmore is director of human resources for Harris Corporation's Information Systems Division. During his 20 years with Harris, Gilmore has provided a wide range of organization design and implementation consulting for both large- and small-scale change projects. Within Harris, he is a recognized corporate practice expert in self-directed work teams. Gilmore has presented on the topic at many local, national, and international conferences, authored several papers on cultural change and high-performance teams, and was a contributor to *Leading Organizational Change* (1997, ASTD). He holds a bachelor's degree from Mount St. Mary's College.

It doesn't matter how fast you're going
if you're going in the wrong direction.
— Ed Rose

Chapter 8

Implementing SDWTs:
Action Steps for Teams

Ed Rose

George Bernard Shaw once wrote that reasonable men adapt to their particular environments and unreasonable men try to adapt the environments to themselves. It follows from that premise, therefore, that all progress results from the efforts of unreasonable men. That may be true in many business situations, but it *does not* apply when it comes to implementing SDWTs. Only the "reasonable" approach—adapting SDWTs to your current business environment rather than adapting your business environment to support SDWTs—will result in success. And, as we have said before, change is not something we do to our employees; it is something that our employees should do. When people have some control of the change process, it is far less intimidating. This chapter presents a six-step process that will assist you in developing and installing SDWTs in your organization.

Key Factors for Success

A common structure is a vital tool for guiding the implementation process. Success depends on the following six key factors:

1. *Commitment*—Team members see themselves as belonging to a team rather than operating independently as individuals. They place group goals above their personal goals. This is where something as small as allowing a team to adopt its own team name helps to bond its members.

2. *Trust*—Team members trust each other to honor their commitments, maintain confidences, support each other, and conform to group norms.

3. *Purpose*—The team understands its role in the organization. Team members feel a sense of ownership and understand how they make a difference. Therein lie the intrinsic motivation factors—autonomy, task significance, and feedback. Autonomy is ownership; through task significance and feedback, people know how their work affects the organization. Remember that the objective here is to define the big picture—the organization's purpose and its future direction—and how the team fits into the picture and supports company core values.

4. *Communication*—Clear, unambiguous communications are vital for success in any venture. Communication refers to the nature of interactions within and outside the team, and to the way that members handle conflict, decision making, and day-to-day interactions. Communication also promotes intrinsic motivation by giving feedback to the workers. For example, Harris plants have monthly all-employee communication meetings in which staff managers share company performance data with employees and the floor is open to any type of questions from employees. Each self-managed team has a bulletin board for posting its activities, and at some plants each team gives a semiannual report to the steering committee. Many plants are using the company intranet to share information among teams and across shifts.

5. *Involvement*—Everyone has a role on the team. Despite their differences, team members must feel a sense of partnership with each other. Contributions are respected and solicited, and a real consensus is established before committing the team to action.

6. *Process orientation*—Once a team has a clear sense of purpose, it must have a process or means for accomplishing its goals. The

process should include problem-solving tools, planning techniques, regular meetings, meeting agendas and minutes, and accepted ways of dealing with problems.

Implementing SDWTs in Six Steps

Using the previous six key factors, Harris developed a six-step process to follow in initiating SDWTs, and now uses it as the basis for SDWT development and implementation. The steps offer a framework for answering the following six questions:

1. Do we know why we exist as a team?
2. What is our vision for the future?
3. What are our goals for the team?
4. What will be our strategies and tactics for reaching our goals?
5. What will be each member's role and responsibilities?
6. What standards and norms will we follow as a team?

Answering those questions will give you an insight into how the team views itself and will enable you to guide the team toward its vision by identifying both potential training issues and support issues that the team raises. As always, use this process as a guide, not a dogmatic recipe, for developing SDWTs to fit *your* environment.

Step 1: Define the Purpose of the Team

1. Ask, why do we exist as a team? The team reviews its role in the organization. How does the team contribute to the company's success? The team develops a *purpose statement* (some people refer to it as a "charter") from these data. Exhibit 2.1 (p. 30) includes a team purpose statement. *Note:* The differing terminology you will encounter from various teaming resources is common. What is important is understanding the terminology and then using consistent terminology within your organization.

2. Ask, what products or services do we produce? The team identifies the product or service that it provides to the organization. The answer is the basis for creating shared responsibility for results.

3. Ask, who are our customers and suppliers? Every team is a supplier, either for internal or external customers. Every team also has internal or external suppliers (Figure 8.1). "Who uses our team's output? What are their needs?" Use Worksheet 8.1 to list suppliers, customers, input, and output.

4. Select a team leader or team coordinator. Select a team recorder.

5. Agree on normal meeting times. Sixty minutes is a good limit for weekly meetings. Also agree on a quorum. Everyone should attend the meetings unless there is an emergency, and if a quorum is not present, major issues should be tabled.

Step 2: Write a Team Vision Statement

Ask the following questions:

- Where are we going as a team?
- How do we want our customers to perceive us?
- How will we know when we have achieved our vision?
- What will the team look like in its ultimate form?
- What will our environment look and feel like if we are accomplishing our vision?

Figure 8.1
Internal Suppliers and Customers

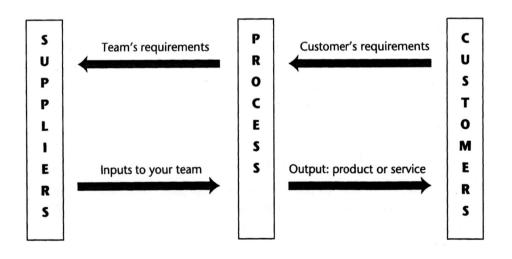

Worksheet 8.1
Identification of Suppliers and Customers

Identification of Suppliers and Customers			
Suppliers	Input	Team Output	Customers

Notes:

_____

_____

_____

Purpose Statement:

_____

_____

_____

When the team has agreed on the answers, the team has a shared vision of the future. There are many methods and techniques for developing a vision statement. Each organization should use whatever it finds most effective, but the vision must be a clear statement that is understood by everyone.

The vision statement is a statement of purpose, direction, and excellence that incorporates the team's existing functions and its view for a future state of excellence. Therefore, the vision statement stretches beyond current performance. The vision also reflects the needs of the team's external and internal customers. Finally, it should instill a feeling of pride in the team members because it represents their identity. Here is the Harris Semiconductor vision statement:

> *To be our customers' first choice for semiconductors used in their new-generation products and systems.*

Each team should develop a vision statement for posting on the team's bulletin board. It also should define observable behaviors (critical success factors, or behaviors that would be observed after the team had achieved its vision) that characterize the environment defined by the vision. Listing those behaviors enables the team to measure its progress toward its vision. After rating the specific critical behaviors, the team can work on those that are keeping it from its vision. Use Worksheet 8.2 to record all of those factors. That process allows the team to work actively toward reaching its vision. With those data, the team is ready to define its goals.

Evaluate your vision statement against the following criteria:

- Does the vision statement include what you do, whom you serve, your desired level of quality and efficiency, issues of responsiveness and professionalism, and so forth?

- Does the vision accurately represent the hopes and direction of the team?

- Is the vision a permanent, comprehensive statement that reflects the organization's values, culture, and environment?

- Does the vision affect all of the team's functions and the areas of activity?

- Is the vision concise, clear, and understandable?

Don't dictate a vision statement to the team. Allow it to grow through this process. If you do not feel the vision statement the team generates is adequate, you may choose to ask the team a few critical questions to lead them toward a better statement, but if it remains satisfied with the statement, allow the team to keep it and learn on its own. Don't try to force your vision on team members!

Vision Statement

Team _____

Date _____

Team's Vision:

Team's Critical Success Factors	Dates	Rating
1.		
2.		
3.		
4.		
5.		
6.		
7.		
8.		

Rating: + = doing it; 0 = weak; − = nonexistent

Step 3: Define the Goals

Ask the following questions:

- What do our customers expect of us?
- What are the actions required to reach our vision? Garner this information from rating observable critical success factor behaviors.
- How will we measure our progress?
- How will we measure customer satisfaction?
- How do we define quality?
- What is quality on our team? How do we measure it?
- What are customer expectations? (Remember that management is a customer, so its expectations are to be included.)

Teams answer those questions and then generate a written set of goals. The goals focus on reaching the vision by working on critical success factors that have weak ratings. Use Worksheet 8.3 to prepare a set of goals, using the critical success factors established in Worksheet 8.2.

Step 4: Identify Strategies and Tactics to Reach the Goals

The team must ask itself, "How will the team accomplish its goals? What are the team boundaries?" Each team must have this information to begin its journey. Exhibit 8.1 presents some sample boundaries set by management. Each organization should develop boundaries that are consistent with its culture and policies. As the team's skills and knowledge increase, the boundaries can change.

The team must identify the information it needs to perform its daily functions. Use Worksheet 8.4 to identify the data needed and determine where and how the team will gather it. The team must identify with whom it interacts and decides how to handle those interactions in the future. Use Worksheet 8.5 to compile that information. Teams also must identify what support they need and any issues they might have with current or future support. Use Worksheet 8.6 to record that information. When the team has answered all of those questions, it is ready to finalize its roles and responsibilities.

Worksheet 8.3
Team Goals

Team Goals			
Team _____			
Date _____			
Team's Critical Success Factor	How Are We Doing? (pick up the rating from Worksheet 8.2)	Actions to Improve Factor	Responsible Team Member
1.			
2.			
3.			
4.			
5.			
6.			
7.			
8.			

Step 5: Delineate Roles and Responsibilities

To begin this fifth step in the SDWT implementation process, the team should answer these questions:

- What tasks being done by others should the team assume?

Exhibit 8.1
Sample Team Boundaries Set by Management

1. No brick and mortar.
2. No overtime.
3. Can't change work schedule (shift hours).
4. Can identify performance problems.
5. Can schedule breaks and vacations.
6. Can solicit customer feedback.
7. Can involve customers in improvement projects.
8. Can propose training plans.

Worksheet 8.4
Team's Information Requirements

Team's Information Requirements			
Team Issue	What Do We Need?	Who Will Supply It?	How Will We Get It?
1.			
2.			
3.			
4.			

- Who is responsible for those tasks now?
- When will the transfer of roles and responsibilities occur?

Roles and responsibilities usually evolve naturally on a team that is in the strategy and tactics stage. Step 5 defines a plan for the formal transfer

Worksheet 8.5
Team's Interaction Responsibilities

Team's Interaction Responsibilities				
With Whom Do We Interact?	Reason for Interaction	Method of Interaction	Current Responsibilities	Planned Responsibilities

Worksheet 8.6
Team's Support System

Team's Support System				
Activity	Location	Function	Support Required	Issues

of specific responsibilities from management and support parties to the team. Teams that have appropriate training can, for example, assume maintenance responsibilities. Committing this to a plan is helpful both to management and to the team who decide at the outset what to transfer and when to do so. Exhibit 8.2 is a sample worksheet for tracking the transfer of roles and responsibilities. For a discussion of how to assign the

Exhibit 8.2

Sample SDWT Responsibility Transfer Worksheet

SDWT Responsibility Transfer Worksheet					
Issues	Who Is Responsible Now?	Transfer Phase (enter phase number)	Shared Responsibility	Management Retains Responsibility	Team Owns Responsibility
Schedule vacation	supervisor	1			X
Determine and plan overtime	supervisor	3	X		
Schedule production	supervisor	2			X
Train new members	supervisor	2			X
Hire new members	supervisor	4*			X
Handle discipline	supervisor	4*			X
Maintain records	supervisor	1			X
Conduct performance appraisals	supervisor	4*			
Authorizes work orders	manager	4		X–supervisor	

*Emphasis is on proper training for these issues.

responsibilities of leadership, see the sidebar "Team Leadership: Star Concept or Shared Responsibilities" starting on page 109.

Step 6: Set Standards, Norms, and Expectations

The team should answer these questions:

- How will we make decisions as a team?

Team Leadership: Star Concept or Shared Responsibilities

Our experience tells us that sharing the leadership on a team is more effective than using a sole team leader. What usually occurs is that the team leader will behave just like a supervisor, thus creating another level of management, and will want more money because of the increased responsibility. With the shared leadership model, team members all participate and feel more satisfaction from the new structure because of their new roles. Some quiet team members may become more assertive when given a team coordinator role. Listed below are some examples of roles that we commonly use on teams. These are not meant to form an exhaustive list. Teams can use them as a guide and develop new ones that meet their specific needs. Remember that the main focus is to transfer responsibility from the supervisor or others whom the team will control. Team implementation step 5, delineating roles and responsibilities, usually is a good place to start planning your coordinator roles. Use the accompanying worksheet to identify roles and responsibilities in your company.

Meeting Coordinator: Prepares agenda, schedules meeting room for use, provides structure, brings meeting minutes and needed presentations to enable a smooth meeting to occur, and informs teams of meeting changes.

Administrative Coordinator: Coordinates vacations and ensures area has enough members to perform to team goals; makes team aware of key meetings and assists with any needed preparations, including development of team presentations for monthly meetings; gets answers to questions involving team overtime, compensatory time, or other issues related to hours worked.

Training Coordinator: Maintains skills matrix; coordinates needed training for SPC, certifications, and team-related activities; works with training resources, other coordinators, or appropriate individuals to ensure that training needs are met.

Systems Coordinator: Performs or ensures that SPC/logbook audits are accomplished; assists with responses to quality control, international standards, and military audits; is responsible for distribution and review of internal process notices and engineering change notices.

Product Coordinator: Responsible for passdowns, hot lot status, interface to other areas such as advanced process design, and other teams on that shift; attends regularly scheduled meetings and any other forums to discuss tactical fabrication strategy.

(continued on next page)

Team Leadership: Star Concept or Shared Responsibilities *(Continued)*

Equipment Coordinator: Monitors equipment status periodically and checks on impaired equipment after two days; checks to see that calibration stickers are up to date; ensures timely preventive maintenance.

Total Productive Maintenance Coordinator: Acts as interface with support teams to ensure flow of TPM-related information to the team; serves as team point person on TPM projects and communicates results to nonteam members.

Team Roles Worksheet

Team Roles		
Coordinator Title	**Responsibilities**	**Training Required**

- How will we manage conflict on our team?
- What will we value as a team?

Many of the behaviors and techniques involved in this step are introduced to teams early in the process. A framework for relationships is critical to any team's success. Ultimate success (that is, team synergy) depends on balancing task accomplishment and interpersonal relationships.

During the vision-defining step, team members identified observable team behaviors that they value. Members must be comfortable in dealing with change and adapting new team behaviors that support effective interpersonal relationships.

During setup of the teaming environment, the subject of trust will come up frequently. Trust is the foundation of all human relationships (see the levels of trust in Figure 8.2), and a team environment is all about relationships. Consider a diverse workforce and the traditional interactions between management and labor. Also consider the interactions among the employees. When you do this, you start to understand the

Figure 8.2
Levels of Trust

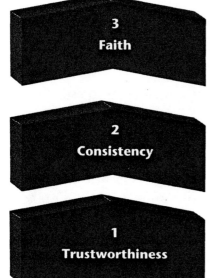

Level 3 – Faith:
Goes beyond facts
Team members experience this level of trust when they can answer "Yes" to the three key questions. At this level, trust has become an integral part of the relationship. Members freely open up to each other. This level of trust is based on the faith they have in each other's conduct in all interpersonal interactions.

Level 2 – Consistency:
Members can be counted on
Team members have developed collaborative relationships through their trustworthiness. This provides a strong base that insulates the relationship from collapsing under difficult conditions.

Level 1 – Trustworthiness:
Building reliability; openness; integrity
Team member's characteristics and attributes that lead to trust, i.e., integrity, reliability, and openness that allow them to build trusting relationships with other team members.

complexity of implementing a team environment. Like a relationship, no team can be successful without trust. Coach Lou Holtz of the University of Notre Dame used three key questions to test for team relationships:

1. Can I trust you?
2. Do you care about me?
3. Are you committed to excellence?

When team members can answer yes to those key questions, they are well on their way to becoming an effective team. Teams must develop effective behaviors to create a strong foundation for team development. At Harris's Palm Bay plant, teams used Covey's *The Seven Habits of Highly Effective People* (1989) as the foundation for all team behaviors. If team members develop those basic habits, they can answer yes to Holtz's key questions.

There are many techniques to help teams develop effective interpersonal behaviors. Encouraging members to change individual behaviors to match the five synergy-producing habits discussed below should create a solid foundation for interpersonal success. If members believe in and use those habits, they can develop an effective teaming environment. Trainers at the Palm Bay plant made small, laminated cards with the five habits printed on them and asked team members to refer to the cards during team sessions. That technique was very effective. They also developed numerous experiential learning activities to enable teams to learn by doing (Rose and Buckley, 1999).

Five Habits of Effective Teams

We believe that the five habits discussed below are essential to establishing synergy on a team.

Habit 1: Think Win-Win

Most employees think only in terms of "winning." On first thought, that sounds pretty healthy. "We won! We got our way. At last!" But take that statement out of the macro level and the original win could end as a loss, depending on who the collective "we" is. Does that proclamation of victory refer to a battle with a customer over a reliability specification? No one ever really wins a fight with a customer. Did "we" win a price war? Price competition is often a last resort to gain or keep market share and the winner is often the company willing to lose the most. Does it refer to a relationship where one person won a point over another? In all of those examples, was there also a loser? Did the customer concur with the win? Did the cost structure have a business ripple effect? How did the other person feel when "we" won our point of view? By winning, what did we give up? What did the win cost everyone involved?

In a compromise, both sides agree to lose equally. The outcome is fair, but no one is really happy. A win-win mindset, by contrast, can yield immense benefits. All participants have to share a vision or goal and adopt each others' issues as their own. That sharing generates trust in a cooperative, not a competitive, environment. Then everybody becomes "we," and "we" win collectively.

Team members should look immediately for the win-win outcome for the benefit of the company. That may mean members do not always get what they want individually in the short term, but it ensures their long-term interests.

It is rare that anyone wins a civil war; the whole country usually loses. It's the same with business organizations as with countries. The United Parcel Service strike in August 1997 showed why organization members must think win-win. The union members prevailed in many parts of their agenda, such as higher pay, but the strike wreaked untold havoc for customers who relied on UPS for shipments and deliveries. An article in *The Wall Street Journal* noted, "As these customers dig out from under piles of inventory and tote up lost sales of summer goods, many are vowing to make sure they're no longer captive to UPS" (Matthews and Deogun, 1997). Some business that went to the U.S. Postal Service and Federal Express during the strike will never return to UPS. "Federal Express expects to keep as much as 25 percent of the approximately 850,000 additional packages it delivered each day during the [UPS] shutdown," *The Wall Street Journal* reported. When the strike ended, UPS laid off thousands of employees because of the expected permanent loss of market share. That result supports neither the union's goal of creating and preserving jobs for its members, nor management's goal of increasing profits for its shareholders. Did the union win or did everybody at UPS lose?

In addressing conflicting agendas, Bishop (1998) wrote, "The best way to secure union jobs is to strengthen the business. All company stakeholders have the same long-term interests" (p. 31). Again, all participants need to share a vision or goal, and adopt each others' issues as their own.

Habit 2: Share Mutual Respect

Mutual respect is another building block for a trusting, cooperative, noncompetitive team environment. It *sounds* self-explanatory, but why do so many issues crop up around it?

Miriam Webster's Collegiate Dictionary, 10th Edition, defines "mutual" as that which is "directed by each toward the other." That's very straightforward. "Respect," however, has several meanings, and everyone probably has his or her own interpretation.

How do we make those two simple words useful tools for building trust? A key principle is maintaining team members' self-esteem. Harris teams are trained to focus on the issue, not the person. When there is a problem, why add conflict by blaming someone or focusing on personalities? The team must look for a problem's root cause in order to solve it. A statement such as, "That stupid engineer didn't move the product" only fuels distrust and interpersonal friction; it certainly doesn't help the product move. We would suggest a statement more along these lines: "The product hasn't moved. Why?"

Eaton Corporation, which uses self-managed teams, once used a variant of the ancient Athenian practice of ostracism.[1] For a short time, management let the workforce vote on whether to keep employees who made mistakes or violated company policies. Although it abandoned that practice, Eaton does require teams that make a mistake to explain publicly what happened and how the mistake could have been avoided (Aeppel, 1997). We do not endorse practices that humiliate or embarrass people. Rather, we prefer the following guidance: Praise in public; give constructive criticism in private; and focus on the problem, not the person. Words are powerful. They can make or break a team's efforts to develop the most responsive way to serve customers. We can use them to set a baseline of respect.

The behaviors for which we reward our team members can be summed up by the following key principles that help build a foundation for mutual respect:

1. Maintain and enhance each team member's self-esteem. Don't say anything negative to a team member, even as a joke. Positive feedback is fine, but remember that it's not what one says but how one says it that makes the difference. That generates trust, which is the foundation of all human relationships.

2. Focus on the problem, not the personality. Team members should deal with the issues, not judge each other or others involved in the problem.

Habit 3: Be Proactive

There are three kinds of people: those who make it happen, those who watch it happen, and those who wonder what happened. Those who make it happen create and guide their own destinies. Those who watch it happen, and adapt themselves accordingly, can survive. Those who wonder what happened don't last long in today's dynamic competitive environment.

To react is to act in response to immediate conditions. If life were like a canoe, a reactive person would let the stream carry the canoe at will, accepting events along the way as unavoidable and responding as events occurred. A reactive person or organization watches what happens and then tries to adapt.

A proactive person in life's canoe, however, would map the stream to prepare for hazards like rapids or rocks, and take along a paddle, or a teammate and two paddles. The hazards, expected and prepared for, would be scenery instead of dangers.

Niccolò Machiavelli (1965) compared organizational challenges to tuberculosis. In its early stages, the disease is difficult to recognize but easy to cure. The proactive doctor (or organizational leader) will prevent the disease or cure it before it can cause trouble. In its later stages, the disease is easy to recognize but difficult to cure. A reactive person or organization will not respond to the danger or opportunity until it is obvious to everybody.

A story that Thomas Cleary included in his translation of Sun Tzu's *The Art of War* (1989) also explains that principle. There were three Chinese brothers who were doctors. One brother was famous throughout the land because he cured serious illnesses. The second brother had a reputation only in his village because he cured illnesses before they became serious. Almost no one knew of the third brother for he stopped diseases at their earliest manifestations. It is the same in business: Troubleshooters and problem solvers are famous for rescuing companies from disasters; proactive people who foresee problems and prevent them from developing remain unknown and unheralded.

The proactive mindset includes responsibility for one's attitudes as well as one's actions. Proactive people can choose their responses. In particular, they direct positive energy toward problem solving rather than falling into a negative victim mode. Victims think in these terms:

- if only's ("If only I had found out last week....")
- social drawbacks ("My coach was so inadequate....")
- genetic makeup ("I could hold my temper if I didn't come from a long line of....").

Proactive people focus less on what others say or what happens to them and more on solving the problem at hand. They are accountable for their actions and learn from their experiences. We expect our team members to focus their energies on things that they can control and that will make a difference. Focusing on negative aspects may get them exactly what they do not want in the long run.

Habit 4: Be a Good Listener

Words are fascinating, and the way we interpret them is even more phenomenal. The human brain's basic design equips it to work with pictures and images. In languages that do not use written symbols and characters that clearly represent ideas and pictures (languages such as English), the brain has to convert the words into images, and so there is room for ambiguity, confusion, and misunderstanding.

Many teams are learning to take time to understand before they try to be understood. That is a recommendation from Stephen Covey. Listening with empathy shows interest. Listen for the meaning behind the words, and if you do not understand, ask. Once you've listened, work at being understood. Such a two-way communication channel builds a common ground of trust, which we have already stressed is necessary in any working environment.

Team members need to listen for and understand other team members' points before sharing their own. Some teams have a rule that you can't state your point until you have articulated the sender's point to his or her satisfaction. That is an excellent technique and should become part of a team's internal communication. "Listening to understand" will go a long way in developing effective team communication.

Habit 5: Think in Terms of Synergy

Synergy is like the taste of peanut butter and chocolate together. Each has its own unique taste but together they achieve a unique effect that neither can achieve alone. In synergy, the whole is greater than the sum of its parts. The individual taste characteristics of peanut butter and chocolate blend to form another taste, but despite the blending, both original tastes remain for us to savor. So it is with teams. Every member has his or her individual characteristics. The blending of their differences makes them what they are together. This difference is the ingredient that creates the synergy. The key is to take the differences of each team member and use his or her strengths to compensate for other members' weaknesses—the whole (that is, the team) is greater than the sum of its parts (the individual members).

As with most human activities, keeping things simple is the best policy. Developing those five habits is a simple approach to optimizing interpersonal communication on a team. Materials are available for use in creating short training modules on those habits. An outline of what Harris developed can be found in chapter 5 in the class is called Team Dynamics, and with that outline you can create your own training module. We recommend that all levels of employees who will be dealing with teams receive the training.

Facilitating Team Development

We believe that developing teams requires facilitation to speed implementation. A facilitator should act as the knowledge broker to the teams and to management during the development process. That does not demand an increased head count, but simply an organizational restructuring. It's a good idea to select a champion to coordinate the overall transition.

During the transition, facilitators should delegate responsibilities to the teams when the teams are ready, but they must not abdicate responsibility without providing proper training for their employees. The six-step process we have documented here enables the team to control its own rate of change, and will help it adjust to the overall organizational change process.

Endnote

1. The Athenians could exile a person, usually a politician, for 10 years by voting with *ostrakons,* or pottery shards.

Yesterday's dream is the basis of
tomorrow's reality.
— Ed Rose

Chapter 9

Implementing SDWTs: Action Steps for Management

Ed Rose

Our intent for this chapter is to describe step-by-step action items to provide focus for your self-directed work teams, from defining the vision to completing the implementation. The action items form a basic process, but that process is not an in-all-cases recipe. Joel Barker (1993) called for managers to display paradigm flexibility. Do not lock yourself up in your past experiences. Instead, adapt the approach we offer here to your company's environment, culture, and history, and consider the needs of your product or service. Good luck on your journey: As Vince Lombardi said, "Good luck seems to follow sound preparation."

Step 1: Define Your Situation

There will probably be some uncertainty about what the organization will be like after its transformation. Change management requires that change agents get people to accept changes despite that uncertainty. The change agent can reduce uncertainty by answering these questions:

- Where do you want to lead the organization?[1]

- What benefits do you expect from the organizational change?
- How will the change improve your product or service?
- How will changes improve other aspects of the business?
- How can this change be linked to other key initiatives underway in the organization?

Write out your answers and be ready to adjust your approach after getting input from your employees.

Step 2: Meet with the Change Management Team

The next step is to orient the people who will lead the change. That team should include the organization's upper management, the people who report to the CEO. Many managers probably know something about SDWTs and autonomous work groups, but they may have garnered that information from different sources and may favor different approaches. All approaches probably are valid, but the change leadership team should agree on a common approach. The approach should be flexible enough to take care of differing needs within the organization, but individual approaches must be similar enough to avoid confusing employees. We recommend that a training orientation session be conducted with the management team. *In Action: Developing High-Performance Work Teams* by Jones and Beyerlein (ASTD, 1998) provides additional guidance for this step.

Sample Format for a Two-Day Management Orientation Session

The session's goals are to define a shared clear vision of the desired change and to create a steering committee that will lead the change process. The meeting should be held offsite—a big step toward getting participants' undivided attention.

Topic Agenda

1. What is a SDWT? (see chapter 1)

a. history

b. what others are doing

c. leaders' vision of SDWT (see chapter 2)

2. Organization as systems of work

   a. technical and human systems (see chapter 7)

   b. examples of other companies with similar product or services that have made or are making the transition

   c. pitfalls of implementation (see chapter 10)

   d. introduction of a change model (use the example in chapter 4 or make your own)

3. Working (breakout) sessions during which participants decide the following:

   a. What will be our strategy going forward?

   b. What type of team structure will work within our company? (see chapter 1)

   c. How can we implement this change based on our change model? (see chapters 3 and 4)

   d. How will leadership be handled during the implementation process? (see chapter 6)

4. Form a steering committee

   a. decide how many members to include

   b. decide if hourly employees and union members will be involved (Remember: Involve those whom the change affects.) (see chapter 4)

5. Develop a shared vision of the new organizational change called SDWTs (see chapter 7).

6. Identify four key measurements that will show clearly how implementation of SDWTs has affected business results significantly (for example, on-time delivery, customer service, factory cycle time, and absenteeism). The steering committee may be the best group to establish and track those measures.

7. Decide on a type of recognition system to use with the teams (see Tools for Trainers, part 1).

Step 3: Let the Steering Committee Assume the Leadership Role

The steering committee should take on the leadership role in the change process, providing the linkage between senior management and individual departments that are adopting SDWTs. In small operations, the steering committee may be the senior management staff with key representatives from the rest of the organization. These are actions to be taken by the steering committee:

1. Establish the design principles for the SDWTs (see chapter 7).

2. Recognize the effect change will have on employees and plan for a controlled implementation (see chapter 4).

3. Assess your current organization.

4. Benchmark other companies that use SDWTs for information about their transition and experience using the structure. Study at least two organizations, or as many as your current business environment will allow. (See the sidebar titled "Site Visits: Informal Benchmarking" [beginning on page 129] for information about benchmarking and for questions that will elicit useful experiential advice about preparing for, installing, and using a self-directed teams approach.)

5. Determine what support is required for the change process.

6. Establish an implementation team for each department involved.

7. Empower each department's implementation team to design and develop SDWTs that meet the vision that the steering committee has defined (see chapter 7). Empower each team to adjust the approach to suit its department, within boundaries set by the steering committee.

8. Monitor progress, problems, and lessons learned to create a continuous cycle of learn–adjust–learn–adjust.

9. Answer the following questions:

    a. What type of training will the move to SDWTs require? (see chapter 5)

    b. How will we support training?

c. Can the organization dedicate the required resources to this training?

d. Will each department provide time for the teams to meet weekly?

e. Are there physical facilities for the teams to hold their meetings?

f. How will we facilitate the change?
   - Will we use additional facilitators?
   - Where will the facilitators come from?
   - Will our plan be successful without facilitation resources?

   The answers to those three questions will be obvious after several benchmarking trips or discussions with others who have made the journey. It's important to note that, although additional resources are required to facilitate the change process, those resources can come from a restructuring of existing resources within the organization.

g. How will the organization's history affect the change? Remember that change will take place in the context of *your* organization's individual culture.

h. Who will be responsible for the training?
   - What type of training will the team members receive? (see chapter 5)
   - How will the training be delivered?

i. How will we know whether the teams are making a difference?

j. What type of communication system will facilitate the exchange of information?

10. Create systems that will provide teams with the correct information to do their jobs.

11. Identify to what extent the following systems need to be changed to support the SDWT concept:
    - company policies
    - hiring
    - compensation
    - promotions
    - appraisal systems.

Step 4: Train and Equip the Implementation Team

All implementation team members need training on the concepts of SDWTs. They will develop action plans for their departments' implementation and define boundaries and expectations for their departments. They should identify any roadblocks to successful implementation and take action to overcome them. To prepare and support the implementation team, management will have to take the following actions:

1. Supply the team with
   - a vision of the new structure
   - expectations and boundaries
   - team constraints
   - as much information as the team can handle. (see chapters 7 and 8)
2. Conduct special training sessions with the firstline supervisors.
   a. Share the vision with supervisors and let them know where they fit.
   b. Share all the information you have.
   c. Let each supervisor know what role he or she will play in the change process and beyond. Be prepared to talk about their futures. Remember that supervisors may feel threatened by this change process.
3. Decide how the employees will be trained on the concept of SDWTs.
4. Choose the structure for the implementation process. (Chapters 4 and 5 will be useful here.)

Team Structure: Management Actions

Actions suggested here are based on the department-specific boundaries and expectations supplied by the implementation team. If the design team decides on this process, look at chapter 8 for step-by-step guidance.

1. Review boundaries and expectations. Organize a product or service and ensure that a clear focus of responsibilities exists. What type of leadership will the teams use?
2. Describe the team's support system.

3. Define each team member's role and encourage job flexibility.

4. Decide how the team will be measured? Will management or the team define the measurements?

5. Ensure that teams have process-oriented measurements at the work-unit level—for example, cost, timeliness, quality.

A foundation for SDWTs should put the team members in control of their work environment. Management must define boundaries and expectations but, within that framework, the team runs its own little business. Workable team structures enable members to plan, schedule, improve, and coordinate products or services for their work areas. It is vital to equip the team members with the skills needed to perform in those new areas. Do not limit training to the task behaviors on a team or to specific job-related skills; interpersonal skills development and group dynamics are equally important.

Remember that most employees have had no experience working in teams. Sports teams may be an important factor in American culture and they may provide great anecdotal examples of specific team behaviors, but watching isn't doing! Management must train the team members.

Step 5: Supervisors Take Action to Support Teams

Managers and supervisors must be comfortable with letting go of their authority, and team members must be comfortable with accepting responsibility. Supervisors should receive orientation training on SDWTs, or be given a copy of this book, and they should understand what upper management expects from them in the SDWT structure.

1. Identify how upper management sees the supervisors' job responsibilities in the future.

2. Seek a commitment for a level of supervisory support during the transition period.

3. Understand fully what this new team-based structure is intending to accomplish.

4. Identify (along with the team) what responsibilities will be transferred to the team (see chapter 8, Exhibit 8.2).

5. Help the team identify what type of training it needs.

6. Supervisors should schedule themselves for facilitator training.

7. Plan for supervisory roles shifting from command and control to consult and coach.

8. Develop a clear understanding of what empowerment means (see chapters 1 and 4).

Step 6: Train the Entire Workforce in the Concept of SDWTs

The six-step process described in chapter 8 is a helpful guide for training your workforce. Below is a detailed description of a four-hour workshop intended to prepare workers for SDWT transition. It will serve as a model for you to use in creating one that suits your particular environment. Several other workshops available from ASTD will achieve the same results. The SDWT Game (see Tools for Trainers, page 166) also will provide a hands-on learning experience.

Sample Workshop: Building Effective Self-Directed Work Teams

This is a hands-on learning experience that shows the benefits of teamwork over those of directive behavior. The philosophy behind the workshop design follows a Confucian maxim:

Tell me—I'll forget.
Show me—I'll remember.
Involve me—I'll understand.

That people learn best by doing is a basic training principle. The workshop simulates first a traditional manufacturing environment and then a team-based culture. Each team will

- work through the six-step change process:
  1. define the team's purpose
  2. write a vision statement
  3. define the goals
  4. identify strategies and tactics
  5. delineate team roles and responsibilities
  6. set standards, norms, and expectations

- experience the supervisor's transition to a coach, facilitator, and disseminator of information.
- develop a new understanding of how support groups can work effectively as team members.
- learn the importance of balancing relationship behaviors and task behaviors on the team.
- experience personally the benefits of teamwork.
- learn various training techniques that can be adapted to most organizations.
- learn by doing.

Workshop Description

Participants work in a simulated manufacturing environment. First, they build a product with direction from supervision and engineering—a traditional approach to manufacturing. Then each team will work through the six-step SDWT implementation process, set up its own work unit, and perform the operation again. This participatory workshop offers creative ideas you can use in training, including several magic tricks. It is an excellent standalone team-building exercise with many options. In this workshop, we assemble a Googolplex item,[2] but any physical simulation of factory work can be used.

Purpose

This workshop shows the power of teams and supplies a simple process for focusing a team's energy in the right direction. A diverse audience can attend the session. What participants learn and take from the workshop is limited only by their innovative abilities.

Instructional Methodology

Instructors will present information and then allow participants to use it in the simulation. A debriefing will follow each step.

Sample Agenda

8:00–9:15 a.m.

- Make introductions, review objectives, and identify participant expectations.

- Set the stage for the exercise by describing the company and selecting a supervisor and an engineer.
- Brief the supervisor and the engineer on their task and roles.
- Have the class build the product with direction from the supervisor and the engineer (15 minutes).
- Debrief participants.

9:15–9:45 a.m.

- Present transition information—changing to a team-based culture.
- Review "Four Terrible Truths" (Stayer and Belasco, 1993):
  1. Success is the enemy; what got us here will not get us there in the future.
  2. I am the problem (Head Buffalo mentality).
  3. For things to change, I have to change first. If you keep going where you are going, you will get where you are headed.
  4. The boss is not the boss; the customer is.
- Review handouts that include the core materials to be shared with the managers.
- Show the short motivational video *Do Right II,* featuring Lou Holtz, football coach at the University of Notre Dame.[3]

9:45–10:00 a.m.   Break

10:00–11:20 a.m.

- Guide each team through the six-step SDWT implementation process and give them the chance to re-engineer the work process and methods.

11:20–11:35 a.m.

- Each team will build the product by implementing their team management system.

11:35–12:00 noon

- Discuss the differences between the two experiences, answering these questions:
  1. Did the directive approach to production seem familiar?

2. What can we learn from this hands-on workshop?

3. Can we apply any of this learning at the plant?

4. Did the six-step team implementation process help? Why? Why not?

Site Visits: Informal Benchmarking

By definition, benchmarking is setting a standard against which to make comparative judgments and evaluate measures. It requires careful observation and recording of qualitative and quantitative data. Benchmarking a company's production process would require flowcharting its methods. For our purposes that focus on gleaning experiential advice from organizations that have planned for and implemented SDWTs, we recommend less formal industrial visits. During each visit, ask questions about the host company's process and experience with teams and share your own perspectives. Use the questions that follow and others of your own to elicit pertinent teaming information.

1. What process did you follow to develop self-directed work teams?
2. If you changed to nontraditional pay systems (for example, skill-based pay), how did you do it and what does the new compensation system look like?
3. Did support personnel change their reporting relationship from traditional, functional reporting to reporting into the self-directed work team?
4. If you have a union or employee association, how did it participate in the change to SDWTs? Did you enter a partnership agreement with your union or association that allowed flexibility to change existing contracts midterm?
5. How do you measure teams?
6. How often do the teams meet?
7. How many people are on a team?
8. What are the steps and what was the time frame of the evolutionary process to empower your teams?
9. What process does the team use in hiring? In firing?
10. What kind of training programs do the team members and team leaders require?
11. How do teams handle disciplinary problems?

(continued on next page)

Site Visits: Informal Benchmarking (continued)

12. Are the team leaders and team members paid the same?
13. Do team members view team leaders as supervisors?
14. Do the team leader positions rotate? What has been the response to that rotation?
15. In rotation, are team leaders paid more than other team members are paid?
16. How is compensation awarded within the team?
17. What procedure is in place for overtime, vacation, and doctors' appointments? Is the procedure working?
18. What is your ratio of employees per coach/facilitator?
19. What training have your coaches/facilitators had?
20. What are your requirements to become a coach/facilitator? How do you staff these procedures?
21. What is your pay structure for coaches?
22. What does your organizational structure look like?
23. Do you have a team of coaches working together, such as a coaches council?
24. How are the facilitators selected?
25. What is the manager's role on the team?
26. How do you handle negativity within the team?
27. How do you keep your team motivated?
28. Do teams have budget responsibility? How does the manager's role work with this?
29. How do you deal with conflict that arises among supervisors, employees, and upper management about the failures that occurred in the process of SDWT implementation?
30. How do you define success?
31. How has the supervisor's role changed?
32. What are the teams responsible for? Do they control quality?
33. What is the organizational structure? Have you decreased your levels of management?
34. To whom does the team report?
35. Are team members cross-trained? Can they do all jobs? What team training do you provide?

Endnotes

1. The following are useful guides for defining your vision: *Succeeding As a Self-Directed Work Team—20 Important Questions Answered,* Ann Harper and Bob Harper, published by MW Corp., New York, 1992; *Quality Management Report* (video series), *SMWT Essentials: How to Make SMWT Work,* produced by Juran Institute, September-October 1995, vol. II, no. 2.

2. Available from Arlington-Hews, Inc., Box 94580, Richmond, BC, Canada.

3. Available from the Washington Speaker's Bureau Video Corporation, Box 25407, Alexandria, VA 22313.

Chapter 10

Ensuring Success, Avoiding the Pitfalls

Ed Rose and Steve Buckley

We believe that by identifying in advance pitfalls and weaknesses in designing and implementing SDWTs, we equip ourselves to overcome them. That approach helps get the teams through the change process successfully. In this chapter we will discuss your role as change agent, and share some of the challenges encountered at Harris Semiconductor. The material will also address studies of autonomy and work team productivity. Understanding the issues that other organizations have faced will provide you an understanding of the facilitation approach required in your business environment.

The Role of the Team Leader

Louis Martin-Vega, an external consultant, began experimenting with two-person teams at Harris in the late 1980s. Activities focused on just-in-time production and operation support areas. The two-person teams were to be seeds, or catalysts, for the coming changes. When Harris began to introduce SDWTs, members of those seed teams became leaders and facilitators for the new teams.

The dynamics of larger teams present a series of new issues. Two people can work together without an official or informal leader. A larger team requires more formal leadership and coordination, as well as competency in interpersonal skills and conflict resolution. At Harris, SDWTs can range in size from five to 20 members, so leadership was important. The people who had participated in the two-person teams were natural candidates for those leader positions.

By early 1990, SDWTs were active in various fabrication areas at Harris Semiconductor. To identify the problems that the team leaders were finding, the training department kept journals on the meetings of 14 teams. The entries provided valuable insights into the leaders' day-to-day challenges in the change from traditional work structures to SDWTs. Items describing leader "weaknesses" included these:

- inability to involve "silent members"
- inability to control personal conflicts
- lack of meeting agendas and the resulting disorganization
- inability to focus the meeting on problems rather than on the personalities of the team members
- insecurity, or lack of confidence in his or her ability to run a meeting successfully
- inability to control multiple concurrent conversations
- lack of presentation skills
- inability to involve the whole team in the discussion, to a point where part of the team felt "ostracized"
- inability to avoid taking things personally
- inability to delegate work, preferring instead to assume too many tasks himself or herself
- too much reliance on the facilitator
- lack of assertiveness.

The journal-keeping study led to a rigorous reappraisal of the support tools required for team leaders and team members. As a result, Harris developed formal training programs in interpersonal skills, communication and presentation skills, conflict resolution, and time management (see chapter 5). The development of the training classes was an outgrowth of the journaling feedback. All teams received training in running effective meetings. Teams could and did rotate the leader position so that everybody could accept the challenge.

Team Size

Studying the 14 teams' experiences also gave us a good idea of the optimum team size. For example, a team of 30 or more people was unwieldy and could not conduct effective meetings. The team worked better after it split into three smaller groups, each of which focused on a common work area. Typical teams within Harris have six to 12 members—an optimum number.

Problems Experienced with Team Development

At Harris, there were many problems at the beginning of the change process. As has been noted, "Programs-of-the-Month" reduce employees' confidence in management's commitment to the programs it proposes. People wondered, were self-directed teams only one more management fad? Should employees invest effort in something that might be here today and gone tomorrow? Such negative preconceptions about any change process are a major pitfall. The change agent needs to weigh skepticism and resistance to change against the idea's acceptance. Strong feelings of personal security and trust in management will reduce the forces that resist change among employees, so the change leaders must be honest and realistic in presenting the SDWT concept to employees.

The following problems reflect many of the comments from the journals kept at Harris, and are issues that one can expect in any transition to SDWTs.

Unwillingness to Accept Team Concept

Americans recognize the team concept in athletic competitions. Football and basketball players work together to achieve results, but the workplace is more like baseball: Everybody is working toward a similar goal, but a large part of the performance is individual. Teamwork occurs only when one player must throw the ball to another player. In the workplace, the shift from individual performance and responsibility to a team structure can meet with great resistance. The underlying concern can be performance measurement: "I don't want to depend on others for how I'm measured." It can also be social in nature: "I do my job and you do yours." Either way, that can be a major pitfall.

Unwillingness to Participate

Some members let the team know that they are much too busy to accept action items or coordination duties. Others want to get the meetings over with and get back to work. Unwillingness to share responsibility becomes the seed for lack of cohesion. This presents a major challenge for the leader and the facilitator. Remember to focus not on the personalities involved, but on the problems that the team must solve.

The star-pointed organization, which was introduced in chapter 2, assigns specific responsibilities to every team member and avoids burdening the leader with all the work. That approach is fair because everybody has something to do. It also avoids the problem of diluted accountability: "If everybody is responsible, no one is responsible."

Language and Ethnic Differences

Team members with language problems may shy away from participating. Race- and culture-based practices also can contribute to members' lack of involvement. In Japan, the homogeneous society has few if any cultural or linguistic differences, so this issue is not a problem. But in the United States, the diverse cultures both challenge and confer advantages on our work teams. A potential weakness of Japanese culture is that everybody wants to conform, to go with the group—and that overarching desire for harmony can lead to groupthink. Japanese workers may work more smoothly together, but American workers should be less vulnerable to groupthink. Leaders, facilitators, and team members must capitalize on the advantages of their team's cultural mix while strengthening its weak points.

Unwillingness to Share Authority

Supervisors and production group leaders must share their responsibilities with other team members, and that may result in displays of resentment at meetings. Remember that loss of status or power is a strong motive for people to resist change. SDWTs take over many of the supervisor's traditional roles. If change leaders do not handle that transition properly, supervisors and production group leaders will perceive it as a threat. Lack of integration of supervisor–operator teams can result in major roadblocks to team success.

Role Uncertainty: Quality Control

Remember that SDWTs also integrate many of the traditional quality control functions. Workers involved in quality control may be unwilling to participate in a team environment. The traditionally conflicting roles of production and quality control often have fostered separate, hostile organizational structures. Production people see quality control people as the "cops" whose job is to catch them making a bad product. Each group must accept new roles in the SDWT structure. The production workers take responsibility for quality. Instead of serving as inspectors, the quality control people provide technical support. The development of joint "quality/production" SDWTs can be among the greatest benefits of the SDWT structure.

Conflict Between Production and Support Teams

Production workers often resent outside engineers, technicians, and supervisory people who tell them what to do. The company must foster the attitude that the production people who work on the front line add value to the product. Support people don't tell teams what to do; they provide support for the teams.

Placing the production teams as the focus of the organization allows them to achieve the factory's goals. Support teams, managers, engineers, technicians, and facilitators are resources who support the teams.

Lack of Skills

We cannot overemphasize the importance of training. People cannot assume responsibility or exercise authority without having the empowering skills to do so. Do not skimp on training. If team members lack the skills they need to perform, train them.

Perception of Management Commitment

Commitment from the top is the "make or break" issue. Teams must be confident that management is behind them. Lack of management commitment—to anything—is among the surest ways to undercut a program. Remember, don't beat the drums unless you mean it.

All of those concerns and issues that arise naturally as part of the transition to a team structure are process improvement opportunities rather than plan killers. The journey to SDWTs is a journey of continuous improvement for all parties concerned.

Major Pitfalls to Avoid

We have seen how journal entries and team feedback helped Harris Semiconductor identify many pitfalls. Benchmarking by other organizations has revealed additional challenges awaiting conversion to SDWTs. You can learn from those experiences and avoid them in your team development process:

- Lack of understanding about why you need self-managed work teams: Change begins with recognizing the need for it. *Do you know why your group is making this change?*

- Lack of management commitment: Management must "walk the talk" and not revert to the old paradigm of management control. *Is your management committed to the change?*

- Failure to invest resources in the change: Put your money where your mouth is by providing training, guidance, and other necessary resources. *Have necessary resources been committed to support the change?*

- Failure to provide structure and guidance during the SDWT transition: Provide boundaries and design criteria. *Have you prepared a structure and a vision of teams?*

- Pay incentive programs under SDWT can be difficult to administer equally and fairly. They must fit within the financial structure of each business unit. This should not stand in the way of acting and continuing to move the SDWT program forward. *Do your company's pay and incentive policies support SDWT development?*
- Destructive competitiveness among teams: Performance measurements must not encourage teams to undercut each other or hope for each other's failure.[1] Provide coaching and facilitation to promote team development and maturity. *Do you have a plan for overcoming these types of workplace cultural issues?*

Do SDWTs Really Improve Productivity?

Many U.S. organizations have been empowering employees recently, but there have been few experimental studies of the effect of such empowerment on productivity. In 1992, the drive toward SDWTs motivated Candice Logan, at the University of Texas at Austin, to do extensive research to characterize the relationships among work team productivity, team autonomy, and team process effectiveness.

The study recognized the following significant strengths of team-based structures: The team is a resource for improving work methods, teams increase attraction and retention of the workforce, teams increase staffing and flexibility, teams increase concern for quality, and teams increase output. The study showed that the potential benefits of team structure are enormous. High-involvement work designs like SDWTs do not, however, *guarantee* the desired results in any given situation. In describing her research findings before the International Work Team Conference in 1994, Logan said, "An effective work team can achieve a level of synergy and agility that could never be designed by organizational planners and managers. However, a poor self-directed work team would perform worse than a smoothly functioning traditional unit."

SDWTs are not, therefore, panaceas. The concept has its weaknesses, and it does not ensure success. SDWTs can be powerful only if the organization commits the necessary time, resources, and faith. The transition to SDWTs is a major undertaking, and it requires commitment and patience. With those attitudes, the change agents can avoid or overcome the pitfalls and develop successful teams.

Behaviors That Support Structural Change

In making the move to a more productive organizational structure, there is one overriding concept to be recalled: *Management must recognize and reward leadership that encourages teamwork and empowerment.* The performance measurement and recognition system must, therefore, promote the desired behavior.

Managers and change agents should not

- insist on numerous controls.
- continue to reward managers for individual rather than team performance.
- be impatient with the implementation process.
- look for someone to blame.

Those behaviors send strong danger signals to new teams. They can even be a signal to stop and go back to the old methods.

Managers and change agents should

- experiment with new approaches and welcome positive change.
- use outside resources and benchmark other organizations.
- encourage breakthrough thinking and overcome self-limiting paradigms.
- encourage risk-taking and learning from honest mistakes; don't punish people for making such errors.
- encourage employees to take that occasional leap of faith.
- seek creative and novel solutions.
- emphasize even small successes.
- become passionate.
- encourage flexibility.
- emphasize the positive.
- walk the talk.
- de-emphasize symbols of status, such as reserved executive parking spaces, dining areas, and restrooms.
- become resourceful.
- look for root causes.

- use vertical and lateral thinking.
- be aware of all possibilities.
- prevent your strength from becoming your weakness by over-reliance on one or two management techniques or methods.
- encourage insight, intuition, and inquiry.
- get ready for tomorrow by making yourself obsolete before someone does it for you.
- create your own futures by making things happen rather than waiting to see what happens.

There are many ways to create teams within your organization. As we have repeatedly said throughout this book, use our experiences only as a guideline, a place to start. No two work environments are alike so it is impossible to implement an off-the-shelf solution for creating a team environment. Your job is to use the examples provided and innovate with them to fit your particular work model. SDWTs are being used successfully in all kinds of work environments—hospitals, construction companies, banks, insurance firms, and, of course, manufacturing operations. They can be used in any organization where there is a serious commitment to change and enough knowledgeable trainers to facilitate the process.

Endnote

1. An example of a dysfunctional reward system is one that ranks three shifts on productivity. As soon as management rates each shift on its output quantity, it is telling each shift (1) "produce as much as you can—don't stop even if you see a quality problem or a chance for improvement," and (2) "don't cooperate with the other shifts. For example, if a machine starts malfunctioning, don't fix it. Let the next shift find out the hard way." As an organization, be careful what you wish for via your performance measurement system—you might and probably will get it!

Tools for Trainers

If you are going to help people reach their potential, they need to be recognized and rewarded. Everyone needs that.

— Bob Nelson
1001 Ways to Reward
Employees

Part 1

Team Excellence Awards: Structured Recognition for SDWT Success

What follows here is a description of a unique structured recognition process designed to help teams move through the developmental phases of implementing self-directed teams and, at the same time, reduce their frustration and raise their levels of comfort with the changes. The Tuckman model (Tuckman and Jensen, 1977) defines characteristics that any type of team would display during the development process, but it does not offer specific actions for accomplishing a transition to self-directed work teams. That model is only a guide to characteristics and attributes of team development through the four phases of forming, storming, norming, and performing. We developed this awards process tool because we believe that the change to self-managed work teams is more complex than the characteristics and attributes covered in the Tuckman model.

Put very simply, to establish an awards process for your company, decide how you want your fully implemented teams to look and perform, develop a plan to get them to that point, break that plan into four segments, and award teams as they complete each developmental segment.

Awards Process: Underlying Assumptions

There are two assumptions that underlie the development of this awards process:

1. A self-directed work team differs from other types of teams because it is a natural work group. Unlike a team that forms to achieve a goal and then disbands, a SDWT produces a product or service on a continuing basis. The team usually has the authority to take initiatives to achieve certain objectives and has the autonomy to manage its daily work.

2. SDWTs develop like other teams, progressing through Tuckman's phases of forming, storming, norming, and performing. We've broken those developmental stages into their social and technical attributes. Table T.1 lists, by phase, the social and relationship characteristics and attributes. Table T.2 shows the corresponding technical and task behaviors. Worksheets T.1 and T.2 are for you to complete for your teams using Tables T.1 and T.2 as examples. The social model applies to all teams; the technical/task model applies specifically to SDWT development. The technical model was created to depict job-related task development in SDWTs and the model will change according to your work environment. Don't force-fit this structure; use it as a guide.

How the Awards Process Benefits Your Teams

The awards process outlined below offers four benefits that help your teams develop into self-directed work teams.

1. It provides a clear road map to both teams and management for the transition from command-and-control environments to the participatory SDWT structure. Talking with your teams and letting them know where they are going will increase their comfort levels.

2. It provides continuity in implementation. No matter how many teams are starting in your organization, all of them should receive the same training so that all of them will speak the same language. Then if employees change teams, they will not have to

Table T.1
Social Characteristics of Team Development Phases

Phase I: Forming	Phase II: Storming	Phase III: Norming	Phase IV: Performing
• Individuals receive a team orientation. • Members are guarded; there is a lack of trust. • Members think in terms of "I." • Conflict is viewed as negative. • Team skills are low. • Members are confused or frustrated. • Members experience exhilaration with new power and experience. • Members are uncertain about benefits of change. • Supervisor or team leader controls the resources. • Supervisor is the customer. • Structure and guidance come from management. • Concepts are synergy and consensus review. • Establish the code of conduct and select a team name.	• There are conflicts and competing styles. • Conflict is often driven by role uncertainty. • Members feel some stress. • Members still function as individuals who think their solutions are best. • There is little effort to give members feedback. • Primary focus is on task achievement. • Supervisor still controls the resources, but begins yielding some control to the team and provides direction. • Team leader is the customer. • Openness and dialogue among team members is encouraged. • Team begins to accept more responsibility for its behavior.	• Team norms are developing; roles become more certain. • Members value harmony and begin to think in terms of "we." They feel good about working together. • Members display trust and supportive behavior. • Members are flexible and adaptive to changes. • Conflicts are handled with a collaborating style. • Communication is open and honest. • Members give constructive feedback to each other. • Primary focus is on the internal customer. • Team is growing in task and process maturity. • Critical thinking is still developing. • Team is becoming independent of the leader/supervisor.	• Team is self-managing. • Team is fully responsible for member behavior. • Team can get information on its own. • There is data-based decision making and creativity. • Contribution of team members is highly involved. • Constructive conflict fosters creativity. • Members freely accept appreciation. • High level of trust exists among members. • Members work well, both together and as individuals. • Team is sensitive to both internal and external customers. • Team balances long- and short-term needs. • Team controls its resources. • Primary focus is on customer satisfaction. • There is no defensiveness.

learn a new approach. The awards program provides the same general approach to each team. The sample criteria provide training, coaching, and guidance to both management and teams.

3. It provides an objective basis for each team to know where it is in the team development process, and for management to rate each team's progress against an objective standard. Surveys can be used, but they are time consuming and the teams can skew

Worksheet T.1
Social Characteristics of Your Organization's Team Development

Social Characteristics of Team Development			
Phase I: Forming	Phase II: Storming	Phase III: Norming	Phase IV: Performing

the actual results by answering the survey in a way that tells management what it wants to hear.

4. It sets lucid expectations for the teams. Clear, unambiguous expectations play a key role in the change from command-and-control to participatory management. It is crucial to involve the people whom the change affects. Again, change should be some-

Table T.2
Technical Characteristics of Team Development Phases

Phase I: Forming	Phase II: Storming	Phase III: Norming	Phase IV: Performing
• Management supplies the output goals. • Management defines team responsibilities. • Measurement systems are provided for the team to learn. • The task is shown to the team. • Team requires coaching in task accomplishment. • Shared responsibility must be developed. • Team must have the required data and resources. • Management sets the decision boundaries and authority limits. • Team structure is formalized. • Orientation is toward the customer.	• Team member roles are defined. • Team focuses on achieving goals. • Team sets up a communication structure. • Technical skills matrix is defined. • Team's decision-making boundaries are expanded. • Internal and external customer expectations are defined. • Cross-training is done to help meet team needs. • Team assumes ownership of its goals. • Team applies SPC, JIT, TPM, and similar tools. • Team develops product dispositioning skills and routine trouble-shooting skills. • Team controls and monitors member participation in team activities.	• Team consistently achieves goals. • Team controls most of the required resources. • Team performs nonroutine trouble-shooting. • Team fully understands decision boundaries. • Team sets quality improvement goals. • Team is capable of making procedural changes. • Team makes disposition decisions. • Team schedules required training. • Team interviews and selects new members. • Members coach each other and give performance feedback.	• Team's technical competencies are at 85 percent or more. • Team performs its own training. • Team controls all aspects of quality, monitors and corrects performance, and adjusts the process (self-control). • Team can change specifications. • Team solves technical problems. • Team performs all routine and preventive maintenance. • Team orders supplies and materials. • Team controls its budget and inventory. • Team is responsible for internal discipline. • Team dispositions product that is on hold. • Team performs designed experiments to improve quality and productivity. • Team controls all related resources.

thing employees do, not something that is done to them. The first step is to let them know what management wants and expects. Unambiguous expectations also guide management's assignment of resources to support the change process.

Worksheet T.2
Technical Characteristics of Your Organization's Team Development

Technical Characteristics of Team Development			
Phase I: Forming	**Phase II: Storming**	**Phase III: Norming**	**Phase IV: Performing**

Award Levels

There are four award categories in our Team Excellence Awards program: bronze, silver, gold, and platinum. Each team receives a plaque that displays its name and team motto. When an award level is reached, the team is given a bronze, silver, gold, or platinum plate to attach to the plaque. Each award level's goals are described briefly below. To define the criteria for each award, we used the Tuckman model, the six-step team implementation process outlined in chapter 8, and key plant metrics that are likely to improve when the new organizational structure is in place. Table T.3 presents the six implementation steps in the form of critical questions to answer. Use Worksheet T.3 to develop your own end product and identify what your teams must accomplish or from and to what they must transition. Table T.4 presents an example of key plant metrics. Use that sample to identify metrics that are pivotal in your organization (Worksheet T.4).

The following explanations of the four award levels use as their bases the team development goals for each phase of implementation. Remember that teams, like growing children, progress differently.

Level 1—Bronze Award

This developmental level is the "directed stage" because the team still focuses on the supervisor as the center of power. The team receives basic interpersonal training that introduces members to the team concept and to expectations for the journey to SDWTs. Chapter 5 described the training classes suggested for this level of team development. Local implementation teams decide what classes are necessary at each award level.

Table T.3
Six-Step Process for SDWT Development

Step	Critical Question
1. Define the team's purpose.	Why do we exist as a team?
2. Write a team vision statement.	What do we want to look like as a team in the future?
3. Define the goals and objectives.	What goals and objectives will we need in place to reach our vision?
4. Identify strategies and tactics.	What strategies and tactics will be implemented to reach our goals and objectives?
5. Delineate team roles and responsibilities.	What roles and responsibilities and what support systems are needed for us to function successfully as a team?
6. Set standards, norms, and expectations	What will guide our development and behavior in this new work environment?

Worksheet T.3
Six-Step Process for Your SDWT Development

Six-Step Process for SDWT Development	
Step	**Answer to Critical Question**
1. Define the team's purpose.	
2. Write a team vision statement.	
3. Define the goals and objectives.	
4. Identify strategies and tactics.	
5. Delineate team roles and responsibilities.	
6. Set standards, norms, and expectations.	

Table T.4
Sample Key Plant Metrics

Metric	Definition
On-time delivery	Orders delivered on or before due date
Customer acceptance rate	Measures the quality of our product
Gap analysis	Indicates how well we satisfy customer needs and expectations
Factory cycle time	Time between order placement and shipment

Worksheet T.4
Key Plant Metrics for Your Organization

Key Plant Metrics	
Metric	**Definition**

The team should know its role in the organization and have a clear vision of where it wants to go in the next five years. Those two understandings are steps 1 and 2 in the six-step team implementation process. All team members are encouraged to attend a workshop about the change to SDWTs. It is important to define a good baseline for the training. Level 1 training is the key to reducing the frustration in the change process and to improving each team member's comfort level.

Level 2—Silver Award

The supervisor is beginning to move away from the center of power and team members are beginning to act as leaders or star coordinators (see chapter 2). This is the "functional stage" because the team is accepting new responsibilities within its defined boundaries. Additional training classes are offered to meet the requirements for this level. The team should begin to select goals that enable it to realize its vision. It should also have strategies and tactics in place to achieve those goals. Clear roles and responsibilities should be identified for the change. The team should know what responsibilities it will assume, and when that will happen. The team defines a system for tracking productivity improvements and aligns the system to key plant metrics.

Level 3—Gold Award

This level is the "empowered phase." The leader or star coordinator has more control, and the supervisors are assuming coach and facilitator roles. With the star concept, the leader position can rotate among members and team members share responsibilities. The team is expected to have systems in place to monitor quality, cost, and productivity.

Level 4—Platinum Award

At this development level, the team is self-directed. The supervisor is now completely in the coach/facilitator role. The team is performing 85 to 95 percent of their day-to-day activities without the intervention of support personnel. In some organizations, a team may even hire and fire personnel and control their own budgets. At this stage, the team does what the supervisor did, within boundaries. Supervisors had limits on their authority, and teams must conform to boundaries, too.

Award Criteria

The criteria we present here should be used only as guidelines for your establishing criteria that serve your organization's needs. The procedure for teams' applying for and receiving awards should be kept very simple. We recommend that each team submit a form showing how it met a level's criteria. You should establish an informal review procedure, and don't make it complicated. Present the award at a meeting with key members of the organization present. The presentation meeting is a valuable organizational communication tool because management learns about issues that teams faced during specific stages of their development.

Level 1—Bronze Award Criteria (Directed)—1.0 Year

At this first stage of team development, the supervisor is still the center of power.

1. Eighty percent of the team has attended Phase I training classes on the following topics: team dynamics, TQM problem solving and goal setting, and building effective SDWTs. The goal of that basic training is to get employees started on the path to self-direction. Organizations should decide their core training requirements at this level.

2. The team has used problem-solving techniques to complete two improvement projects that address problems within its area of responsibility.
   - The team has formally presented a project to the implementation team.
   - The team has submitted a written document to the respective area managers, detailing the process that the team used at each step and the results it achieved, including data on the most significant improvements.

This requirement ensures that all employees are familiar with and can use the organization's particular problem-solving process.

3. Eighty percent of scheduled meetings have occurred. This criterion stresses the importance of meetings even when other activities appear more critical. It also underscores management's commitment to the development process. Management does not expect teams to cancel meetings to push production numbers.

4. The team has achieved an average of 90 percent attendance at the team meetings for the quarter preceding nomination. This requirement stresses the importance of meeting attendance.

5. Every meeting has an agenda. This is a basic requirement for effective meetings.

6. The team records and keeps minutes. This criterion reinforces the idea of keeping meeting records.

7. Team members are familiar with monthly production schedules and quality goals, and the team measures its weekly performance against them. This effort helps team members assume responsibility for measuring their own performance. It is a basic step

in self-control, which involves knowing the requirements, getting feedback to measure performance, and responding to the feedback.

8. The team has agreed on a code of conduct and/or team agreement for meetings (see Exhibit T.1 as an example). This effort is a basic step in team formation.

9. The team has defined its vision and purpose statements.

10. The team has identified its customer and supplier relationships and requirements.

11. The team documents and tracks administrative and quality issues and provides feedback to its members. This criterion helps the team accept ownership for those issues and outcomes.

Exhibit T.1
Sample Code of Conduct for Team Members

- Listen to and respect the views of other members.
- Be open and encourage the ideas of others.
- Take responsibility for the team's progress.
- Maintain a friendly attitude.
- Strive for enthusiasm.
- Everyone is equal.
- Give others a chance to express themselves, even if it means less personal participation.
- Remember that the only stupid question is the one not asked.
- Pay attention and avoid disruptive behavior.
- Attend meetings regularly and participate in discussions.
- Carry out assignments on schedule.
- Ensure that credit is given to those to whom it is due.
- Show thanks and appreciation to nonmembers who give assistance.
- Adhere to team agreements.
- Take responsibility for housekeeping.

---

12. The team has developed detailed job descriptions for each of the star positions in a work cell, when appropriate (see Exhibit 2.2 as an example). This process helps the team create its own future, and it improves the team's comfort with change.

Exhibit T.2 is a sample bronze award application form. In the first column are the award criteria defined by the organization. The team fills in the date each requirement was completed. A representative of the next level of authority, as identified by the steering committee, verifies completion by initialing the third column. You can use Worksheet T.5 to create application forms for all award levels in your organization. Define the criteria for each level.

Level 2—Silver Award Criteria (Functional)—Total of 2.0 Years

A team will be ready for level 2, the functional stage, about one year after its organization. At that point, the supervisor is starting to move toward a coach/facilitator role and the team is into its journey of development.

1. The team has identified the values and standards necessary to achieve its vision.

2. The team has developed improvement goals that use its values and standards. That ensures that the team is working toward its vision.

3. Eighty percent of the team members have completed the Phase II training classes that management decided are necessary at each level. Teams request additional training if they feel they need it. The course topics include effective communication, conflict management, and giving constructive feedback.

4. The team has developed a team information and access list to help it complete tasks more effectively (see Worksheet 8.4).

5. The team has identified its interaction responsibilities with customers, suppliers, and support groups (see Worksheet 8.5).

6. The team has identified the support system that it needs (see Worksheet 8.6).

Exhibit T.2

Sample Bronze Award Application

Bronze Award Application		
Award Criteria	**Date Completed**	**Verification**
Eighty percent of the team has attended the following Phase I training classes: team dynamics, TQM problem solving and goal setting, building SDWTs.		
The team has used problem-solving techniques to complete two area improvement projects.		
Eighty percent of scheduled meetings have occurred.		
The team has achieved an average of 90 percent attendance at team meetings for the quarter preceding nomination.		
Every meeting has an agenda.		
The team records and keeps minutes.		
Team members are familiar with monthly production schedules and quality goals. The team measures its weekly performance against production and quality goals.		
The team has agreed on a code of conduct or team agreement for meetings.		
The team has written its vision and purpose statements.		
The team has identified its customer and supplier relationships and requirements.		
The team documents and tracks administrative and quality issues and provides feedback to its members.		
The team has developed detailed job descriptions for each of the star positions in a work cell, when appropriate.		

7. The team has identified the tasks and responsibilities that it will assume and those that management will maintain. There is also a schedule for the transfer (see Exhibit 8.2).

Award Application		
Award Criteria	**Date Completed**	**Verification**

8. The team has set up a system to track its productivity and quality improvements. This effort helps the team focus on key plant metrics.

9. A baseline has been established for team productivity and quality (annual operating plan goals). This activity also focuses the team on key plant metrics.

10. The team has established a baseline for cycle time (a key plant metric), and it tracks improvements.

Level 3—Gold Award Criteria (Empowered)—Total of 3.5 Years

When the team progresses into level 3, the empowered level, it is taking on more responsibility and the supervisor has moved further into the coach/facilitator role.

1. The team fully displays the attitude that supports team harmony (as rated by the responsible management representative). This includes thinking "we," not "I." The goal is to have team members working together.

2. The team ensures that its members understand and fulfill their roles. Are the roles from the bronze level being performed?

3. The team has defined norms, which show themselves in trust, support, openness, and communication among team members (as rated by the management representative). Is the training in interpersonal relationships working?

4. The team is now responsible for 50 percent of all day-to-day activities (with a final goal of 85 percent).

5. The team has set up a mechanism for daily and monthly intrateam communications. Are communication systems in place?

6. The team has set up cost-control systems in its functional area and continues to focus on key metrics.

7. The team focuses on cross-training to ensure its flexibility to meet varying demands.

Level 4—Platinum Award Criteria (Self-Directed)—Total of 5.5 Years

At level 4, the team is fully self-managed. It accomplishes 85 to 90 percent of its daily activities without outside support. Management has transferred all responsibilities to the work unit, as planned at silver award level 2. This requirement ensures follow-through on transferring responsibilities.

1. Productivity and quality indexes are in place and reflect improvement. That helps tie the team's performance to plant metrics.
2. The team is fully multifunctional (multiskilled) (see social and technical models, Table T.1). This criterion ensures that the team can handle daily issues without additional support.
3. The team is 85 percent self-sufficient in the technical competencies. The goal is for the team to require less outside support for technical problems.
4. The team performs its own skills training.
5. The team now controls all aspects of quality and is responsible for quality.
6. The team controls all related resources, with the authority and boundaries that once belonged to the supervisor.
7. The team handles all disciplinary issues, with the authority and boundaries that once belonged to the supervisor.
8. The team reviews members of the rewards team, as specified by team and management. Again, the team has the authority and boundaries that once belonged to the supervisor.
9. All support functions are in place. Ensure follow-up from level 2 requirements.
10. All decisions are based on data. Can the team make sound decisions?
11. High levels of trust and synergy are evident, as rated by both facilitator and team members. Are members working together?
12. Customer satisfaction has improved.

Administration of the Awards Process

Management Responsibilities

1. A steering committee from each department guides the overall process. It approves the criteria and changes them where appropriate to meet the needs of the department.

2. The plant operations steering committee provides the resources for the awards program. The training department facilitates the process and handles new training requirements during the transition.

3. The steering committee reviews all award level applications. It makes a formal presentation to each team member at a meeting with senior-level managers present. This aspect of the awards program is a valuable step in building positive management–employee relations. The managers discuss the teams' development with the employees.

Team Member Responsibilities

1. The team reviews the award criteria and develops a plan to meet the requirements. The team secures whatever support it needs. The training department facilitators help as needed.

2. The team prepares its own application form and submits it to a member of management for preliminary approval. The form goes to the steering committee for final approval. This system is based on trust. The team members know the award criteria; there are no extensive recordkeeping or tracking systems to verify application claims. Management trusts the team members to meet the requirements for development based on their desire to improve, not to receive an award.

Team Excellence Awards Overview

This awards tool should have given you a good understanding of a structured recognition system. The program is a valuable supporting tool for SDWT development. Remember, however, that you must adapt the approach to meet *your* organization's needs. Management in your company must define expectations for the teams and develop criteria that work in your specific business environment. Some basic team development criteria will be the same from organization to organization, but others will differ noticeably. It is helpful to identify a champion in your organization to lead your change. As we noted earlier, management must supply the resources if the teams are to succeed.

A structured recognition process can become the focal point for the SDWT implementation. It provides built-in goals and milestones and ensures continuity within the organization. The program relies on trust between the team and management.

As you know, the process of change involves trial and error, false starts, and blind curves. Leaders must create an environment where it's okay to make mistakes and start over without fingers being pointed and blame assigned. A structured recognition process reduces trial and error and eliminates some blind curves. It creates an environment where learning and creativity flourish, boosts employees' comfort levels, and reduces everyone's frustration.

You can see your organization as it is
and ask, "Why?" or you can see your
organization like it should be and ask,
"Why not?"

— Ed Rose

Part 2

Activities and Interventions

Self-directed work teams are not a quick fix or a "Program-of-the-Month." They require genuine and sustained commitment from all levels of management. As a training professional, you are an asset to an organization that understands the value of teams. It can take more than five years to complete the transition to SDWTs as integrated facets of your organizational culture.

In your role as change agent in the transition you will need interventions and activities to convey your message. The tools in this section will help you teach others the value of team work. The authors have used them successfully with various clients around the world to emphasize key learning points. The exercises require only a few materials and set-ups and can be valuable assets to you in your training role as a change agent.

1. *SDWT Game:* This experiential learning activity helps participants to understand some of the basic concepts of SDWTs (chapter 9).

2. *The Leadership Game:* With this experiential learning activity, participants experience the dynamics of leadership firsthand (chapter 6).

3. *Power of Vision:* This physical activity gives the participants the experience of succeeding after mentally visualizing improved performance. This can be used effectively when you are discussing vision and its value to the process (chapter 7).

4. *Trust: The Foundation of All Effective Teamwork:* This is an illusion that prompts a discussion of the levels of trust (chapter 8).

5. *Can We All Just Agree?:* This is an experiential intervention in which members try to reach consensus in a fun activity. Use it when explaining the meaning of consensus and how to attain it (chapter 5).

Those few activities and attention-grabbers will help you illustrate in a training session or presentation the key learning points covered in the chapters cited parenthetically. As a trainer you certainly can find numerous connections to other learning points.

The SDWT Game[1]

Overview: Using only the materials provided, participants must pick up a tennis ball and move it from point A (the starting point) to point B without dropping it. The work unit must act in unison to accomplish the task. Managers will direct all activities in the first round, with the workers blindfolded if desired. During the second round, the workers remove their blindfolds and perform the task without management direction.

Objectives:

- to simulate the traditional management model
- to simulate keeping the workers in the dark with blindfolds
- to simulate an empowered workforce
- to show that with the proper information and training, the worker can perform successfully.

Group size:

- minimum of seven people (six workers and one manager) per team
- maximum of 13 (with six workers, six managers, and one senior manager) per team

- six workers are required per team, but management member numbers can fluctuate
- if you have more than 13 people, extras can serve as observers/spotters.

Environment: Indoors or outdoors

Suggested time: 50 to 60 minutes (20 to 30 minutes for the exercise and 30 minutes for a debriefing session). The time required for the exercise depends on the distance and obstacles between point A and point B (trees, fences, doorways, steps, and so forth).

Materials needed:

- one tennis ball
- one ring, approximately two inches in diameter, that will hold the ball (Figure T.1)
- six pieces of string or twine 15 inches in length, tied to the ring (Figure T.1)
- six blindfolds (optional)
- a method for timing the initiative
- a copy of the SDWT Game handout (Exhibit T.3).

Procedure:

1. Prior to beginning the activity, prepare the carrying sling as shown and lay it on the ground or floor with the ball on it (this spot will be point A).

2. Select point B and mark it somehow. The distance between point A and point B will vary according to the obstacles in the path between them.

3. Divide the participants into teams and either appoint the manager(s) for a team or have the team select them. *Optional:* Blindfold the six workers. It may be best not to use blindfolds until you have run this activity a few times and are comfortable with it. If all six workers are blindfolded, you will need six managers; if blindfolds are not used, you will need only one manager.

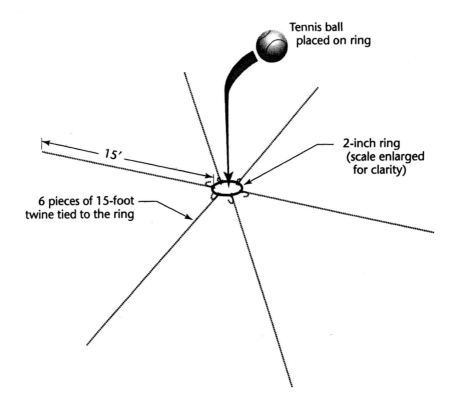

Tennis ball
placed on ring

2-inch ring
(scale enlarged
for clarity)

15'

6 pieces of 15-foot
twine tied to the ring

4. Greet the group by saying, "Welcome to the Acme Mining Company. Unfortunately, there has been a terrible rockslide in our Number 7 mineshaft. You have been hired to do some very important work for us. Your manager will fill you in on the details."

5. Give the manager(s) a copy of the handout. *Be sure to tell them that managers cannot assist workers physically.*

6. Tell manager(s) that they may begin the activity when they are through planning.

7. Observe and time the activity, and take notes.

8. Let the group know when there are 15, 10, and five minutes left.

9. The transfer is complete when the tennis ball ("C4") is set in the point B dropoff zone and the pickup device is removed. Allow the group to celebrate if successful.

10. Debrief using the following questions:
    - *(to workers)* How was your relationship with management?
    - *(to workers)* How satisfied were you with the way you were led?
    - *(to workers)* Were you good workers?
    - *(to workers)* What interfered with your ability to listen? What did you do to overcome the interference?
    - *(to workers)* Did any of you think of shortening the ropes? Did you share the idea with management? Why or why not?
    - *(to workers)* Did management freely share information with you?
    - *(to managers)* How satisfied were you with the way your workers listened and followed your instructions?
    - *(to managers)* Did you think of shortening the ropes? Did any workers suggest this? Did you follow that suggestion?

- *(to workers and managers)* In what ways does this exercise parallel your current environment? What insights can you take back to your day-to-day environment?
- *(to workers and managers)* Would a SDWT have the same problems you experienced? (The answer here is no. In the traditional command-and-control environment, workers are kept in the dark [blindfolds] and the managers have the knowledge but do not share it.)

11. Allow the participants to repeat the task as a SDWT (that is, do it without the blindfolds and with the manager acting as a coach).

12. Debrief after this activity with the following questions directed at all participants:
    - What difference did you experience?
    - How would this way of operating work in your organization?
    - This was only a simulation, but can you see any comparisons to your work environment?

The Leadership Game²

Overview: Using a deck of playing cards, each of three teams must maximize profit (points earned in a Heart War) with specific card choices. Each team identifies itself with a suit—spades, clubs, or diamonds—and then selects a leader to make play decisions. Each team earns points based on the face value of the cards it wins. Each team's aim should be to obtain 30 points in heart-faced cards.

Objectives:
- to experience the effects of leadership on a team
- to demonstrate various dynamics of leader selection
- to demonstrate how consideration for others is important.

Group size: three teams with three to five members on each team

Environment: Indoors with round tables—a set-up that allows all participants to view what is taking place

Suggested time: 60 to 75 minutes (30 to 45 minutes for the exercise and 30 minutes for a debriefing session)

Materials needed: one standard deck of playing cards for every three teams

Procedure:

1. Prior to the activity, separate the deck of cards into the four suits—hearts, diamonds, spades, and clubs.

2. Form the participants into three teams. Let them self-select or choose teams based on your objectives for the day.

3. Give each of the three teams a suit of cards—diamonds, spades, or clubs. Keep the heart suit cards for yourself.

4. Explain that participants will be playing a game in which the objective is to get 30 points worth of heart cards.

5. Explain the following guidelines:

   • Each team will select a team member to make the decision about when to play a card. He or she will be the team leader.

   • The team gets points each time it wins the hand. A hand is won by the team that plays the card with the highest value (ace = 14 points, king = 13, queen = 12, jack = 11, 10 = 10, and so on).

   • The number of points awarded for each hand is equal to the value of the heart card won in that round.

   • Participants can talk to members of other teams only before play starts.

   • No one may talk during a hand.

   • Teams may not give their cards to other teams once they have won them.

6. Encourage team leaders to negotiate with each other prior to the beginning of the game. They will decide whether to play a card that wins the hand. (You need to encourage them only if they do not do it on their own.)

7. Begin the game and tell the leaders to select their first card and to place their selection face down on the table.

8. Lay your card (the heart) face up on the table and instruct the team leaders to turn their cards over. The team with the highest-value card wins the round and gets the number of points represented by the heart card.

9. Continue in this manner for four more cards.

10. After you play the fifth card, allow team leaders to confer with their team members and discuss their progress. The team leaders can also discuss progress with the other team leaders. *Note:* The objective is to let the teams figure out that if they work together they can all meet their goal of 30 points. There is no benefit to them to get more than 30 points. If they fight with each other, one or more teams may lose; if they collaborate, they will all meet their goals.

11. After a few minutes, tell the teams it's time to start again and play the remaining eight cards. *Note:* If you plan to play two rounds, then don't break during the first round. Wait until the second round to allow teams to confer.

12. After all the cards have been played, total up the number of heart points for each team.

13. Conduct a debriefing session using the following questions:
    - *(if the teams selected their own members):* How did you select your teams? On what criteria did you base the selection?
    - How did your team select its leader?
    - What goals did your team decide on?
    - Did your team discuss the overall task?
    - Who decided on the strategy, the team or leader?
    - Did your team leader negotiate with other team leaders?
    - How did you feel as a team member? Did you feel that your role was limited?
    - Were there any attempts to cooperate with the other teams?
    - Did any team members disagree with the leader? If so, did they communicate this to the leader?
    - In what ways does this exercise parallel your current environment? What insights can you take back to your day-to-day environment?

The Power of Vision

Overview: Participants are given a physical activity to perform and are asked to measure the result. They then are asked to establish a goal in their minds beyond that which they achieved initially. Next, they are led through a visualization exercise, and when they attempt the activity again they exceed their previous efforts.

Purpose: This activity can be used to demonstrate the power of visualization.

Procedure:

1. Explain to the participants that you are going to walk them through an exercise that demonstrates the power of visualization.

2. Have the group spread out so that everyone has plenty of room to move their arms.

3. Have participants raise their right arm, holding their palms forward and their fingers and thumb in alignment. (If some of them raise the left arm because they are watching you, give them the old line, "No, your *other* right arm!")

4. Tell them to sight down their arm and to rotate their torsos as far as they can to the right without moving their feet. Have them make a mental note of where they stopped (perhaps by identifying a spot on the wall).

5. Tell them to return to the starting point and to follow the directions you're about to give them, no matter how silly they may feel about it.

6. Have them close their eyes and *visualize* themselves turning to the spot where they stopped the first time, and then turning another 20 percent farther than that.

7. Tell them to return to the starting point and again *visualize* themselves rotating about 30 percent beyond their initial stopping point.

8. Now have them do it again, but this time tell them to *visualize* turning 50 percent past their initial stopping point before they return to the original position.

9. Now have the participants open their eyes, rotate, and see how far they can go—most will be amazed at how much farther they can go than on their initial try.

The message: It is important to visualize your ideas or concepts in your mind's eye. The power of what you see can be critical to success or failure. When implementing a change in an organization, visualize success.

The secret: Sorry, but this is a special Zen Master secret and he told me never to tell anybody. You do, however, have all you need to make this exercise work every time. It might be that this is not actually an illusion or trick, but an actual example of the powers of visualization. What do you think?

TRUST: The Foundation of All Effective Teams

Overview: You pour water from one cup into another and tell the audience that you are going to make the water disappear by waving your hand over it. If you ask the audience, "Do you believe I have made the water disappear?" and someone says "yes," you ask that person if you can prove it to everyone by tilting the cup over his or her head, as a proof of trust in your having done what you promised.

Objective: Used with Figure 8.9, this serves to illustrate the difference between "believing" and "trusting."

Procedure: Gather three plastic cups, two about half-full of drinking water and the third containing the "secret ingredient," slush powder. Pick up one of the cups with water in it. Hold it up and ask, "Do you believe I can make this water disappear?" Someone will surely yell out, "You can drink it," but if no one suggests that, say "I could drink it," and do so. Toss the empty cup away to prove there's no water left in it. Now pick up the other two cups and pour the water from the half-full cup into the cup containing the slush powder. Do it so that everyone can see the water pour from one cup to the other. Turn the emptied cup upside down when you put it back on the table to show the audience that the water really went into the other cup. Wave your hand over the cup you are holding and say, "Do you know what I'm doing? I'm making the water disappear. Does anyone believe me?" Hopefully someone will say "yes" (you can probably get at least one person to agree because of some bonding that might have occurred during the session—look for a friendly face). When someone says he or she believes you, ask if they will trust you to "pour—no, I mean tilt..." the cup over his or her head to demonstrate to everyone that you did make the water disappear. The general response is, "no way!" but some people reason that it's only water and they can't get hurt too bad, so they will allow you to do it. They don't *really* trust you, but they take the gamble nonetheless.

Your point is made when you say, "We all know that no one can make water disappear," as you tilt the cup over the trusting person's head. As an option, simply walk away with the cup and turn it upside down slowly (no water will come out). Be sure to dispose of the cup with the powder in it properly so that no one gets a look at it.

The message: It is easy for someone to say he or she believes you if there is little investment to be made (that is, little personal commitment or little risk). Remember the story about the relative contributions of a chicken and a pig in the making of breakfast—the chicken is involved but the pig is *committed.* Use the levels of trust described in Figure 8.9 to expand your discussion and to support your position. The water example illustrates a leap of faith.

The secret ingredient: Slush powder, a very inexpensive effect that can be purchased from almost any magic shop. Use it according to the directions that accompany it.

Can We All Just Agree?

Overview: Participants are separated into teams and asked to come up with a symbol, sign, or gesture that best represents their team. All teams then gather to display their team's chosen symbol, sign, or gesture to the other teams. The teams then break off again to decide which of the displayed symbols they want to represent the whole group, without communicating with any other team.

Objectives:

- to provide an entertaining way to experience consensus
- to explore how conflicts can develop

- to demonstrate that groups can reach consensus without discussion
- to open a dialog on what consensus means to a team.

Group size: two to 15 people per team with a two-team minimum (works best with four teams)

Physical set-up: Indoors or outdoors. If possible, allow room for teams to separate so they cannot hear or talk with the other teams.

Suggested time: 15 to 30 minutes (five to 10 minutes for the exercise and 15 to 20 minutes for a debriefing session)

Materials needed: none

Procedure:

1. Separate the participants into teams.
2. Identify an area in the room for each team.
3. Allow teams to select a name if they wish.
4. Instruct the participants to come up with a symbol, sign, or gesture that represents them as a team. You may specify that the group relate their choice to their work environments.
5. Tell teams they have five minutes until they must share their choice with the other teams. Make it clear that any gesture must be culturally acceptable.
6. After the five minutes are over, bring all the teams together and have each team, one at a time, demonstrate its symbol, sign, or gesture, and explain why they chose it. This part of the procedure can be fun.
7. Tell participants to return to their teams and decide which of the displayed gestures, symbols, or signs they want to represent the entire group. Give the teams three minutes for this task. Remind them not to talk with members of other teams.
8. Bring the groups together again and ask each team to demonstrate the gesture, symbol, or sign they chose. Again, they must explain why they chose it.
9. If all teams have decided on the same sign, gesture, or symbol, then go onto the debriefing session. Otherwise, continue until

the groups reach full consensus. *Note:* There may be instances when a team will not want to change its position. If the groups are unable to reach an agreement after three additional rounds, stop the activity and proceed to the debriefing session.

10. As the facilitator, you can add pressure by saying, "Our customer requires that we must decide on one symbol, sign, or gesture." Sometimes this motivates teams to rethink their positions because they know that customer expectations are important in the real world.

11. Conduct the debriefing session using the following questions:
    - *(if all the teams reached consensus)* What difficulty did your group have reaching a consensus with the other groups?
    - *(if all the teams did not reach consensus)* What difficulties did you encounter while trying to achieve consensus?
    - *(if all the teams did not reach consensus)* What was the basis for you changing your mind?
    - *(if appropriate)* Why were you unwilling to change your choice?
    - Did anyone dominate the decision making?
    - Are there times that we might reach consensus without talking?
    - In what ways did this exercise violate the basic process of reaching consensus?
    - In what ways does this exercise parallel your current environment? What insights can you take back to your day-to-day environment?

Endnotes

1. Thanks to Jim Cain of Cornell University for his inspiration on this activity.

2. Thanks to Dick Teach of Georgia Tech for the original idea that prompted Ed Rose developing this activity.

References

Aeppel, T. (1997, Sept. 9). "Missing the Boss: Not All Workers Find Idea of Empowerment As Neat as It Sounds." *The Wall Street Journal*, p. A1.

Automotive Industry Action Group. (1995). "Potential Failure Mode and Effects Analysis." http://www.aiag.org.

Barker, J. (1993). "Paradigm Pioneers." Available from Charthouse International Learning Corporation, http://www.charthouse.com

Bishop, R. (1998). "Culture as Foundation." In *Leading the Way to Competitive Excellence: The Harris Mountaintop Case Study* (pp. 25–52), W. Levinson, editor. Milwaukee: ASQC Quality Press.

Covey, S.R. (1989). *The Seven Habits of Highly Effective People.* New York: Simon & Shuster.

Covey, S.R. (1991). *Principle-Centered Leadership.* New York: Summit Books.

Deal, T.E., and A.A. Kennedy. (1982). *Corporate Cultures.* Reading, MA: Addison-Wesley.

Hamel, G., and C.K. Prahalad. (1994). *Competing for the Future.* Boston: Harvard Business School Press.

Imai, M. (1997). *Gemba Kaizen.* New York: McGraw-Hill.

Jones, S., and M. Beyerlein. (1998). *In Action: Developing High-Performance Work Teams.* Alexandria, VA: ASTD Press.

Levinson, W. (1994). *The Way of Strategy*. Milwaukee: ASQC Quality Press.

Levinson, W., and F. Tumbelty. (1997). *SPC Essentials and Productivity Improvement: A Manufacturing Approach*. Milwaukee: ASQC Quality Press.

Levinson, W., and J. Lauffer. (1998). "Paradigm Busters." In *Leading the Way to Competitive Excellence: The Harris Mountaintop Case Study* (pp. 15–23), W. Levinson, editor. Milwaukee: ASQC Quality Press.

Machiavelli, N. (1965). *The Prince*. New York: Airmont.

Matthews, A.W., and N. Deogun. (1997, August 20). "Stung by UPS, Some Shippers Seek Alternatives." *The Wall Street Journal*, pp. B1–B2.

Peters, T. (1987). *Thriving on Chaos*. New York: Harper & Row.

Peters, T. (1988). *Structures for the Year 2000*. Palo Alto, CA: Tom Peters Group.

Peters, T. (1989). "When Surviving Is Not Enough." Presentation to the Cornell Society of Engineers, Ithaca, NY, April 28, 1989.

Rose, E., and S. Buckley. (1999). *50 Ways to Teach Your Learner*. San Francisco: Jossey-Bass/Pfeiffer.

Stayer, R., and J.A. Belasco. (1993). *The Flight of the Buffalo*. New York: Warner Books.

Sun Tzu. (1963). *The Art of War*. Translated by Samuel B. Griffith. New York: Oxford University Press.

Sun Tzu. (1983). *The Art of War*. Translated by James Clavell. New York: Delacorte Press.

Sun Tzu. (1989). *The Art of War*. Translated by Thomas Cleary. Boston: Shambhala Publications. Audiocassette.

Tuckman, B.W., and M.A.C. Jensen. (1997). "Stages of Small-Group Development Revised." *Group and Organizational Studies 2*, 419–427.

Wentz, M. (1998). "Teaming to Win." In *Leading the Way to Competitive Excellence: The Harris Mountaintop Case Study* (pp. 53–87), W. Levinson, editor. Milwaukee: ASQC Quality Press.

Suggested Reading

Cain, J., and B. Jolliff. (1998). *Teamwork & Teamplay*. Dubuque, IA: Kendall Hunt.

Caravaggio, M. (1998). "Total Productive Maintenance." In *Leading the Way to Competitive Excellence: The Harris Mountaintop Case Study* (pp. 117–144), W. Levinson, editor. Milwaukee: ASQC Quality Press.

Clausewitz, C. von. (1976). *On War*. Translated by M. Howard and P. Paret. Princeton, NJ: Princeton University Press.

Covey, S.R. (1996). "Organizational Alignment," *Quality Digest* (March), 21.

Cummings, T.G., S.A. Mohrman, A.M. Mohrman Jr., and G.E. Ledford Jr. (1985). "Organization Design for the Future: A Collaborative Research Approach." In *Doing Research That Is Useful for Theory and Practice*, E.E. Lawler III, A.M. Mohrman Jr., S.A. Mohrman, G.E. Ledford Jr., T.G. Cummings, and Associates, editors. San Francisco: Jossey-Bass.

Davidow, W., and M. Malone. (1992). *The Virtual Corporation*. New York: HarperBusiness.

Duarte, D., and N.T. Snyder. (1999). *Mastering Virtual Teams*. San Francisco: Jossey-Bass.

Feigenbaum, A.V. (1991). *Total Quality Control*. New York: McGraw-Hill.

Fischer, K., and M. Fischer. (1997). *The Distributed Mind*. New York: AMACOM.

Ford, R. (1998). "An Introduction to Harris Semiconductor." In *Leading the Way to Competitive Excellence: The Harris Mountaintop Case Study* (pp. 9–14), W. Levinson, editor. Milwaukee: ASQC Quality Press.

Gies, J. (1991). "Automating the Worker." *American Heritage of Invention and Technology* (Winter), 55–79.

Harper, B., and A. Harper. (1989). *Succeeding as a Self-Directed Work Team*. Croton-on-Hudson, NY: MW Corp.

Hitchcock, D., and M. Willard. (1995). *Why Teams Can Fail and What to Do About It*. Burr Ridge, IL: Irwin.

Imai, M. (1986). *Kaizen*. New York: McGraw-Hill.

Isinger, R. (1996). "Aleksandr Suvorov Won Many Battles, But a Retreat Was the Crowning Achievement of His Military Career." *Military History* (October). http://www.thehistorynet.com/MilitaryHistory/articles/10962_text.htm.

Levinson, W. (1994). *The Way of Strategy*. Milwaukee: ASQC Quality Press.

Levinson, W., editor. (1998). *Leading the Way to Competitive Excellence: The Harris Mountaintop Case Study*. Milwaukee: ASQC Quality Press.

Lipnack, J., and J. Stamps. (1997). *Virtual Teams: Working Across Space, Time and Organization*. New York: John Wiley & Sons.

Longworth, P. (1965). *The Art of Victory*. New York: Holt, Rinehart, and Winston.

Martin-Vega, L. (1988). "Management of Change." Presentation to Harris Semiconductor, Palm Bay, Florida.

Miller, R.B. (1985–1986). Lectures on organizational behavior. Poughkeepsie, NY: Union College.

Murphy, R.E., and W. Levinson. (1996). "Self-Directed Work Teams." Presentation to ASQC Annual Quality Conference, Chicago.

Murphy, R.E., and P. Saxena. (1998). "Synchronous Flow Manufacturing." In *Leading the Way to Competitive Excellence: The Harris Mountaintop Case Study* (pp. 145–185), W. Levinson, editor. Milwaukee: ASQC Quality Press.

Nadler, G., and S. Hibino. (1990). *Breakthrough Thinking: Why We Must Change the Way We Solve Problems, and the Seven Principles to Achieve This.* Rocklin, CA: Prima Publishing and Communications.

Oshry, B. (1995). *Seeing Systems: Unlocking the Mysteries of Organizational Life.* San Francisco: Berrett-Koehler.

Parker, G. (1994). *Cross-Functional Teams: Working with Allies, Enemies and Other Strangers.* San Francisco: Jossey-Bass.

Paterno, J. and B. Asbell. (1989). *Paterno: By the Book.* New York: Berkeley Books.

Purser, R., and S. Cabana. (1998). *The Self-Managing Organization.* New York: Free Press.

Rose, E., S. Gilmore, and R. Odom. (1993). "A Harris Semiconductor Division's Journey to Self-Directed Work Teams." Presentation to the IEEE Technology Symposium, Boston.

Rose, E., S. Gilmore, and R. Odom. (1993). "A Journey to Self-Directed Work Teams with 'TLC.'" Presentation to the ASTD National Conference, Atlanta, GA, September 1992.

Rose, E., S. Gilmore, and R. Odom. (1993). "Six Steps to Building SDWT." *Quality Digest* (December), 29–33.

Rose, E., S. Gilmore, and R. Odom. (1994). "Improving Team Meetings." *Quality Digest* (August), 24–31.

Rose, E., and R. Murphy. (1996). "Theory of Constraints: Best Practices at Harris Semiconductor." Presentation to the Forty-Seventh International Industrial Engineering Conference, Nashville, TN, May 1994.

Rose, E., and R. Odom. (1994). "Climbing the Mountain of Change." Presentation to the Fifth Annual Advanced Semiconductor Manufacturing Conference, Boston, November 1994.

Rose, E., and R. Odom. (1996). "Four Key Ideas for Successfully Implementing Change. Focus: Transitioning to Team Base Management." Presentation to the ASQC Annual Quality Conference, Chicago, May 1996.

Rose, E., R. Odom, R. Dunbar, and J. Hinchman. (1995). "How TOC & TPM Work Together to Build the Quality Toolbox of SDWT." Presentation to ASQC, January 1995.

Rose, E., R. Odom, R. Murphy, and L. Behnke. (1995). "SDWT Requires Tools to Be Successful." Presentation to the Sixth Annual Advanced Semiconductor Manufacturing Conference, Boston, 1995.

Sands, A. (1998). "Customer Contact Teams." In *Leading the Way to Competitive Excellence: The Harris Mountaintop Case Study* (pp. 89–103), W. Levinson, editor. Milwaukee: ASQC Quality Press.

Sands, A. (1998). "Zero Scrap Actions." In *Leading the Way to Competitive Excellence: The Harris Mountaintop Case Study* (pp. 105–115), W. Levinson, editor. Milwaukee: ASQC Quality Press.

Stamps, D. (February 1997). Communities of practice: Learning is social. Training is irrelevant? *Training Magazine 34,* 35–41.

Toffler, A. (1971). *Future Shock.* New York: Bantam Books.

Wenger, E. (July/August 1996). Communities of practice: The social fabric of a learning organization. *Healthcare Forum 39*(4), 20–26.

About the Editors

Ed Rose is currently sector training and recognition manager at Harris Semiconductor in Palm Bay, Florida. He graduated with honors in organizational management from Warner Southern College. He is the author of *Presenting and Training with Magic*, published in 1998 by McGraw-Hill, and *50 Ways to Teach Your Learner: Activities and Interventions for Building High-Performance Work Teams*, published in 1999 by Jossey-Bass/Pfeiffer. He has authored team-building exercises in resource books published by McGraw-Hill and HRD Press. Rose has 32 years' experience in manufacturing, has served as quality examiner for the state of Florida, and has published extensively on the subject of self-directed work teams. He is a corporate practice expert for SDWTs with Harris Corporation. Rose is a frequent presenter at ASTD and the Association for Quality and Participation national conferences and the University of North Texas International Conference on Work Teams, and has presented and conducted workshops in Australia and Europe as well as at local colleges and high schools. He is a member of the International Brotherhood of Magicians and the International Magicians Society, and has played on 15 world championship softball teams and been selected to eight All-World teams over the last 10 years.

Steve Buckley is senior training specialist at Harris Semiconductor in Palm Bay, Florida. He graduated from Indiana Vocational Technical College with a degree in computer programming. He is the editor and publisher of the *Palm Bay Pulse* site newsletter for Harris and edits and designs all manufacturing training materials produced at Harris's Palm Bay facility. He also assisted in the development of Ed Rose's two earlier books, *Presenting and Training with Magic* and *50 Ways to Teach Your Learner: Activities and Interventions for Building High-Performance Work Teams.*

CPSIA information can be obtained at www.ICGtesting.com
Printed in the USA
LVOW051114211111

255811LV00001BA/2/A

9 781562 861292